Communicating
with China

Communicating with China

EDITED BY ROBERT A. KAPP
FOR THE CHINA COUNCIL
OF THE ASIA SOCIETY, INC.

INTERCULTURAL PRESS / CHICAGO

Published by Intercultural Press, Inc.
70 West Hubbard Street
Chicago, Illinois 60610

© 1983 by The Asia Society, Inc.
Library of Congress Catalogue Card Number 82-83999
ISBN 0-933662-51-3

FIRST PRINTING
Printed in the United States of America

The China Council of The Asia Society

The China Council is one of the many programs of The Asia Society, a not-for-profit and nonpolitical educational organization dedicated to deepening American understanding of Asia and to promoting thoughtful trans-Pacific discourse.

The Council was established in 1975 to seek fresh approaches to American public education about Chinese history and contemporary life and about U.S.-China relations. Its programs bring a variety of viewpoints as well as the knowledge and insights of diverse specialists on Chinese affairs to adult audiences throughout the United States.

In the years since its inception it has created a network of regional councils across the country which develop programs to meet local needs and interests. It has also sponsored the publication of a number of educational materials for general and specialized audiences and conducted a program of assistance to print and broadcast journalists.

The China Council draws major support from the National Endowment for the Humanities, the Atlantic Richfield Corporation, the Exxon Corporation, The Henry Luce Foundation and Mr. David Rockefeller. The China Council staff is located at 1785 Massachusetts Avenue, NW, Washington, DC, 20036, Tel.: 202/387-6500.

About the Contributors

Jan Carol Berris is vice president of the National Committee on U.S.-China Relations. She joined the National Committee staff in 1972, after having done graduate work in Chinese studies at the University of Michigan and worked for the United States Information Agency in Hong Kong. Ms. Berris has served as escort for scores of American delegations going to China and Chinese delegations visiting the United States.

Robert A. Kapp is executive director of the Washington State China Relations Council, which facilitates contact and exchange between Washington State and the PRC. He holds a Ph.D. in modern Chinese history from Yale University and has taught at Rice University and the University of Washington.

Timothy Light teaches in the department of East Asian languages and literature at The Ohio State University. He taught at New Asia College in Hong Kong in the early and late 1960s and received his doctorate in linguistics in 1974 from Cornell University. Since then he has taught Chinese language and linguistics at the University of Arizona and Ohio State.

Stanley B. Lubman is a partner in the San Francisco law firm of Heller, Ehrman, White & McAuliffe. For over a decade he has represented American businesses in China. He received his law degree from Columbia University, where he also specialized in Chinese studies, and has taught at the School of Law at the University of California at Berkeley.

Douglas P. Murray is vice president of The East-West Center in Honolulu. He was a representative of The Asia Foundation during the 1960s, president of the National Committee on U.S. China Relations in the early 1970s and director of Stanford University's United States-China Relations Program from 1975 to 1981.

Yao Wei works for the Ministry of Foreign Affairs of the People's Republic of China. He has served as the escort for prominent Americans visiting China, including Edgar Snow and Henry Kissinger. In 1980-81 he was, in turn, a fellow at the Woodrow Wilson International Center for Scholars, Harvard University, and Stanford University.

Acknowledgments

This book began with a friendly panel session in an elegant, stately Connecticut mansion in the perfect New England autumn of 1980. Under the auspices of the China Council of the Asia Society, a group of friends and colleagues in the China field met to hear some papers and discuss the process by which Americans and Chinese in the People's Republic of China communicate with each other.

The panel went well, and the discussion was lively. It seemed easy enough to take the morning's transactions and put out a simple book so that others could share the day's insights and perhaps better conduct their own work with China. I agreed to edit the collection, figuring on a comma here and a new paragraph division there, and we tacitly assumed that the session could be in print inside of six months.

Twenty-one months later, we are ready to go to press. The project resembles its original conception only slightly. Busy authors and editors have reworked and re-reworked their efforts, then waited for months while others did the same. A set of panel papers has become, we hope, a useful little book.

Had our first notions proved practical, we would have needed few if any acknowledgments. But now I have to thank those who have given of themselves in order to put out a publication of real value:

Richard C. Bush, Susan Williams O'Sullivan, and Terry Lum both of the China Council of the Asia Society, for endless assistance in coordinating the progress of the project and making vital editorial contributions; Margaret D. Pusch, President, David S. Hoopes, Editor-in-Chief, of Intercultural Press, for supporting the publication of this material and for further skilled editorial suggestions; Yvonne Hu, Sachiko Kiyabu, and Daisy Kwoh for their calligraphy; Jan Berris, Tim Light, Stan Lubman, Doug Murray, and Yao Wei, our contributors, for, among other things: graceful patience with an amorphous band of editorial critics, flexibility in reconsidering their ideas and their prose, and their lively intellects which made it possible to combine unique personal experiences with the most profound issues of human communication; and finally, The Washington State China Relations Council, for backup assistance to the editor in preparing this volume.

——ROBERT A. KAPP

Contents

Communicating
with China

Introduction

ROBERT A. KAPP

Relations between the United States and the People's Republic of China are maturing rapidly. Twenty-two years passed between the collapse of the American presence on the Chinese mainland in 1949 and the Nixon-Kissinger *demarche* of 1971; already more than a decade has elapsed since that breakthrough. The icy silence of the fifties and sixties, warmed only by the flames of wars-by-proxy and shattered only by bursts of bombast, seemed immutable at the time; in retrospect, it appears as an interruption of a longer, more continuous dialogue. In the future, if the two countries continue to forge deeper and fuller ties, twenty years of alienation may take on an insignificance that few among us, who came of age in the era of hostility, would have dreamed possible.

The tangible, poignant sense of bonds renewed, of opportunities wasted, and of lost time to be made up, overhangs the

1

U.S.-China relationship in the minds of many Americans and Chinese today. The U.S.-China relationship of the 1980s cannot, however, simply pick up where both sides dropped it more than thirty years ago. The Sino-American encounters of the last decade have been of a different order than those the United States and China knew before 1949. Despite China's urgent need for technology and knowledge from abroad, crucial elements of the old picture—the missionary presence, the heavy involvement of U.S. finance in China's modern economic sector, the treaty port system with its accompanying mentalities, the underlying assumption on both sides that China was the weaker participant in a fundamentally unequal relationship—are no longer present. The continuities are there, to be sure; but the fact of the Communist revolution and the changes it has wrought will not go away.

The diplomats, traders, academics, tourists and opportunists who have been building the intricate web of relations over the last decade had to start nearly from scratch. Americans had precious little lore—accumulated practical wisdom rooted in experience—with which to prepare themselves for direct dealings with the People's Republic of China. The academic studies that proliferated during the 1950s and 1960s generally addressed scholarly analytical concerns and represented the kind of detached research that limited their value when the time came for "hands-on" work. Taken together, the articles offered here give evidence of how Sino-American relations have recently matured. They present the opinions of specialists in U.S.-China relations who by this time have gathered a rich store of experience. Five years ago, the experiential base was much thinner; the lore was not available. Today it is, and it should be pondered before and during any serious encounters with counterparts in the People's Republic. To be sure, these essays reveal that frustrations, vexations and mystifications persist in Sino-American interchanges. The translation process, for example, confronts tantalizing ambiguities; these can be rendered less surprising and less damaging (as Ms. Berris points out in her discussion of interpreting), but they will never be completely banished. Most Americans will never internalize the anatomy of the Chinese language; few will grasp the domestic social and bureaucratic environments of their Chinese opposite numbers with enough clarity to affect their own professional decisions.

In short, we have come a long way in a short time—hence this set of essays on down-to-earth problems of language and communication with the PRC. But we have far to go. We hope that *Communicating With China* will stimulate and inform a wide range of readers, from those with no prior direct contact with China to those who have been engaged with Chinese counterparts for years. But the value of this book for readers with no background on China will grow as they do related homework. People who are seeking in the 1980s to forge their first contacts with China, especially in business, must accept the fact that they are not breaking new trails through unexplored territory. Many business people have gone before them, and it makes very good sense to absorb the information and the lore already generated by those who have been at work with China in the recent past. Basic information on the structure of the Chinese government and foreign trade apparatus, for example, or on the political and economic policies of the People's Republic, is readily available and should be mastered. Several organizations in the United States, including The Asia Society's China Council and the National Council for U.S.-China Trade in Washington, D.C., and the National Committee on U.S.-China Relations in New York (as well as the U.S. Commerce Department itself) can point newcomers in the right direction. So, too, can such easily acquired publications as the Commerce Department's *Doing Business with the People's Republic of China*, several up-to-date and highly respected China guidebooks, and even the pamphlets published by major international banks and other commercial-service organizations. *Communicating With China* seeks to present not a manual of procedure, but a set of insights with which to understand some very important cross-cultural experiences implicit in our contacts with the People's Republic of China.

Professor Light gives a sensible and readily-grasped view of the Chinese language itself. On the heavily argued question of whether basic differences in form and function of languages create basic differences in the thinking processes of those who use them, Light replies firmly, "They don't." Jan Carol Berris, of the pioneering National Committee on U.S.-China Relations, draws on her immense experience in the field to analyze the role of the interpreter and to illuminate the social-educational milieu which produces these essential craftsmen. Stanley Lubman distills from years of commercial negotiation with the Chinese some key themes of direct relevance to business people in the China trade. Among his many contributions, Douglas Murray helps us to recognize the dangers of tunnel vision in approaching our own China experiences—of assuming, for instance, that behavior displayed to Americans is displayed *because* they are Americans, instead of recognizing that such behavior is also displayed toward fellow Chinese. Murray's sensitive perceptions approach the levels of sophistication that the best American writers of the 1930s and 1940s, Graham Peck for instance, achieved in their generation.

Finally, Yao Wei's contribution is significant both for what it says and for what it is. We have indeed passed a milestone when a visitor from the People's Republic, who specializes in China's relations with the United States, commits himself to paper for American readers on the question of Sino-American communication. Yao's insights and gentle reminders to

4

Americans as to how the Chinese might perceive *them* are very much to the point. Indeed, a whole separate volume could well be formed around the question of how Americans communicate with other peoples, the Chinese included.

Though this introduction precedes a series of fine articles on vital current topics, I would like to take this opportunity to add a few comments of my own on the problem of Sino-American communication.

First, Americans tend to look at their interactions with foreigners by analyzing the way the other side behaves while paying scant attention to the way they themselves behave. If only the Chinese can overcome bureaucratism; if only the Chinese can erect workable legal frameworks for trade; if only the Chinese can rid themselves of destructive political factionalism—etc. We fall into the habit of viewing the future of U.S.-China relations at all levels in terms of what happens on the other side. Similarly, as in this publication, we scrutinize the way the other side acts or expresses itself or operates in certain circumstances, without asking ourselves how we do those things. People engaged in work with the People's Republic of China owe it to themselves to absorb as much useful background information on China and the Chinese as they possibly can. But they also should ponder American habits, American tendencies, American styles in dealing with foreigners generally and the Chinese in particular. The essays by Yao Wei and Douglas Murray make this point most forcefully, but it deserves a fuller consideration than the scope of this collection permits.

Second, China is, and has been for thousands of years, extremely language-conscious. In traditional culture, mastery of the written word and literacy were the keys to power and status; the written word had a mystique that lent to its possessors an almost priestly quality in the eyes of illiterate commoners.

In the twentieth century, the language has been modernized as a part of China's broader cultural transformation, and literacy has been extended to the masses. In addition, the techniques of propaganda and public information associated with Communist Party practices have had their effects on language and communication in China. Today, literary expression, propaganda, written and oral communication are highly refined; they are situationally specific, often stylized in ways that most Americans fail to recognize, and fraught with political or social significance.

Some of the results are obvious: Americans recognize fairly easily the tendency to repeat platitudes and set-phrases in public dealings with foreigners; they can at times see for themselves that to the Chinese some situations seem to call for an almost operatic rhetoric and others call for low-key unadorned communication. Americans should also remember that, just as choice of words is unconsciously or consciously on the minds of the Chinese with whom they are dealing, they too should choose their words with care. The kind of casual, loose or hyperbolic chatter that Americans like to employ in conversations with their fellows is to be avoided; the Chinese hearer, perhaps because dealing with foreigners has always been a specialized, technically refined art in Chinese culture, is likely even today to take the American's words with a literal-mindedness and seriousness the speaker may not have intended. The time for symbolic statements, posturing, mirth and hyperbole may come (one learns to recognize the appropriate times for verbal flights), but the starting point should be a spare, not particularly colorful language that leaves as little as possible to the inevitably culture-bound imagination of the Chinese listener.

Third, Chinese forms of communication are situationally specific and the language is constantly changing. The turgid, moralistic, officially approved materials in major newspapers and

6

other media of the so-called "big road" differ greatly in both style and content from the unofficial, gossipy communication of the popular "little road." Despite the efforts of twentieth-century cultural reformers to make the written Chinese language more like the spoken idiom, virtually no written Chinese displays the spontaneity and vocabulary of informal spoken Chinese dialogue. Most foreigners most of the time will remain confined to the more official forms of communication and isolated from intimate uses of the language, precisely because they are foreigners. Furthermore, though the assimilation of terms from the scientific and technical *lingua franca* into Chinese represents a step towards firmer communication with Chinese counterparts (a point emphasized below by Mr. Lubman), Chinese language is constantly forming new, domestically generated catchphrases and abbreviations with which even the most up-to-date dictionary cannot stay abreast. Here, it seems to me, Americans must, for their part, keep things simple whenever possible; but they must also realize that they may not be "up" on the latest Chinese vernacular. Since Chinese is a condensed language, with a long tradition of capsule abbreviations of longer formulae, Americans who develop sophisticated communications with Chinese colleagues need to be sensitive to the evolving language of their counterparts and to take in and hold as many of the terms and phrases in current use as possible.

Even though it makes matters more complicated, I must also note that the Chinese recognize in themselves a long-standing proclivity for engaging in empty verbiage. Philosophers and statesmen for millennia have complained that words and reality seem to go their separate ways in China, leaving perhaps literary elegance or complexity but little substantive meaning. The problem has not gone away in the People's Republic. Slogans have often taken the place of meaningful statements; euphonious or ritualistic catchphrases used, like talismans, have dulled the senses of foreigners and Chinese alike. The present is an era of political and economic "pragmatism" in China, but the legacy of the catchphrase and the slogan dies hard, and the task of sorting out the symbolic and ritualistic pronouncements from the more directly meaningful ones will confront Americans in the future. The Chinese, of course, are not alone in manipulating words or sucking the meanings from them before using them: bureaucratese, social-work jargon, "psychobabble" and political sloganeering, to cite just a few parallel examples, are all alive and well in the United States. Again, the advice is offer—and expect—simple, unadorned communication with Chinese counterparts.

The wonder of it all is how well Sino-American communication is doing, given the fundamental language differences, historical and cultural contrast, differing ideological and political systems, and the snafus that most of the authors cheerfully recognize in the essays that follow. With care, patience and sensitivity to readily perceived pitfalls, workable communication is taking place all the time, and with increasing effectiveness. Our aim, after all, is not to have our opposite numbers see things through our own eyes—that is impossible. For most of us the aim is to locate common ground with a minimum of wasted time and effort and, by sharing that ground, to develop effective relationships with Chinese counterparts. That common ground will never be exclusively "made in USA" or "made in PRC," but it is expanding and becoming more stable as the months and years pass. We hope that the articles offered here will help that vital process along.

Face to Face:
American and Chinese Interactions[1]

DOUGLAS P. MURRAY

We found during a recent stay in China that some of our most memorable interactions with Chinese never happened. Curtains were pulled to eat behind, to drive behind, even to view the Yangzi Gorges behind. Served lunch in the aft dining room of the "East is Red #48" river boat from Chongqing to Wuhan, we and forty-odd other foreigners routinely had a wall of cloth pulled over the panoramic windows that would otherwise have framed some of the world's most spectacular scenery. Our initial befuddlement at this seeming madness dissolved quickly as

---

[1]Much of the reflection and drafting for this article occurred during a recent three-month stay in China. The insights of my wife, Peggy Blumenthal, and subsequently of my Stanford colleagues Roy Tsung and Tom Fingar, clarified many thoughts and flagged many errors of interpretation. The remaining flaws are strictly my own doing.

we realized once again that the purpose was not to impede us but to *protect* us—from the mass of Chinese faces outside pressed against the panes to watch our gaggle of brightly attired aliens using chopsticks. (As it was, the curtains were not seamless, and the steady stare of Chinese passengers, one eye at a time, could usually be spotted at the blowing edges.) We were being shielded from rudeness, not from the scenery; we were being "helped," not hindered. But one man's sweet is another man's sour, and the interactions of Americans and Chinese remain bittersweet, largely because each understands so little about the motivations of the other.

The Context of Contact

The protective screen on the Yangzi was only one vivid reminder that the two cultures and political systems approach each other from very different perspectives and seek communication from different premises about social relations. Chinese, for example, traditionally have not cast their nets of civic concern very widely; but those clearly within one's net (family, friends, colleagues, clients) receive all possible protection, nurture and support—and foreign guests receive far more than most. Americans define social responsibilities much more broadly, but we assume they primarily involve regulating our *own* behavior, and worry about others within our purview largely when they are clearly in trouble. Victor Li, in *Law Without Lawyers*, provides a metaphor of the contrasting views of law that applies equally to the wider realm of social order. Americans generally allow each other to walk freely toward the cliff, reluctant to interfere until someone falls off the edge of crime or major deviance, at which point the power of civic or state institutions is rushed to the scene (at least ideally). For Chinese, Li observes, the cliff doesn't exist, being replaced by a long gradual slope; every step people take down the slope toward danger is (again,

10

ideally) countered by supportive hands that try to push them back up to the straight and narrow. Prevention, not cure or punishment, is the primary goal, including prevention of embarrassment and loss of face. Chinese expect support and protection; Americans often resent it.

For Chinese, protection is so highly valued precisely because it has been so hard to come by. The China "liberated" in 1949 was wracked, as Graham Peck noted in *Two Kinds of Time*, by "the savage individualism that had grown so strong during the recent century of national disintegration" and the "anti-social behavior" it engendered. Hence, for thirty years the PRC's socialist system has been attempting to extend through modern ideology and mass institutions the old primary-group values of protection and prevention—to make "serving the people" a *national* imperative and an ingrained ethic, though with only mixed results. Concurrently, the West has become ever more "individualistic," in practice if not in principle. One result of these divergent trends has been a strengthening of the mutual admiration that is so often noted: Chinese (at least the urban educated) widely admiring the freewheeling, resourceful personalities they associate with American democracy and modernity, and we often yearning for the simple virtues of discipline and public purpose we thought we saw in China's idealized welfare state. We each exaggerate the virtues of the other yet rather enjoy the wistful longing for traits we lack and have so little prospect of acquiring. It might well be this underlying mutual admiration that makes the interactions of Chinese and Americans the pleasant experiences they usually are—despite endless frustrations and puzzlements.

Interactions between Americans and Chinese are, of course, just variants of each people's dealings with other cultures generally, not an entirely unique process. Although China's international experience is far longer, America's is much deeper

11

and richer; we are a "new" people whose origins are culturally diverse, for whom international association is relatively commonplace and travel is routine. In contrast, China's foreign dealings have long roots but sparse branches. John Fairbank reminds us that handling foreigners is a refined Chinese art—the highly organized, stylized process associated with things rare, important and rooted in tradition. In *China: The People's Middle Kingdom and the U.S.A.*, Fairbank summarizes "Chinese operating principles for the manipulation of barbarians" that can (or should) be recognized by any reasonably alert American visiting China today. The need to put the best foot forward in dealing with the outside world (*duiwai yinxiang*) remains deeply felt in both private and official circles.[2] But our response should be cautious: when are we experiencing that special treatment and behavior reserved for foreign guests, and when are we simply caught up in China's *own* cultural patterns to which we are not attuned? When are we confronting traits deeply rooted in Chinese culture and when the contemporary hand of authoritarian politics and

---

[2] A glimpse of China's self-conscious concern in receiving foreigners— the flip side of our own "briefings" for China-bound Americans—was provided in March 1981 by Peking's *Worker's Daily*. An article on "things to bear in mind when meeting foreign guests" suggested:

"Avoid political arguments at all costs."

"Don't ask people (especially female guests) how old they are; don't ask how much they earn; don't casually ask what is the price of their clothing and their belongings," because "some words and behavior which we don't mind so much may appear rude . . . to foreigners."

"When you see somebody falling down or having other accidents, you should immediately go forward and help. Never stand aside and laugh."

"After you have been to the washroom, properly secure your belt and button up your pants before you come out."

The article also warned people not to talk too loudly or shout greetings from afar—thus fingering yet another feature of China's social scene. (UPI, *San Francisco Sunday Chronicle and Examiner*, March 15, 1981)

bureaucracy? Most of us can't readily make these distinctions, and they won't be attempted here.

Our interactions are not, however, a simple extension of our vastly different cultures and politics. While reflecting both, they also vary independently—with time, place, age, education, language skills and certainly with personality. After 1971, the contacts renewed with such enthusiasm through Ping-Pong were a study in formal hospitality, decorum and mutual acceptance. But since 1978 or so, with frenetic speed, our cultural, economic, academic and tourist encounters have assumed a more open, warts-and-all quality, due in large part to the domestic relaxation within China that probably will (but might not) continue. The greater directness, even bluntness, that we find when travelling south from Peking through China's "mediterranean" provinces is paralleled by Chinese encounters with the hectic rough-and-tumble of New York after the more easy-going hospitality of San Francisco and/or the Midwest. China's urban elite, with whom we customarily interact, present a very different face than do the worker and peasant masses whom we see largely from a distance. Foreigners who speak Chinese can find China equally, perhaps even more, puzzling than do those who must travel under the protective wing of English-speaking guides, though for different and more complex reasons; and in our quest to fathom and communicate with Chinese society our encounters with China's English-speaking (the "modern" elite) can be as misleading as they are rewarding. Any sampling of letters from the hundreds of Americans working in the PRC demonstrates that China remains a massive Rorschach test that can evoke the full range of our long-time love-hate sentiments toward things Chinese. There is no consistent pattern to the interactions of Americans and Chinese, just as neither country has a uniform culture. But there are parameters that help in understanding those variations. The way we extend or avoid socially protec-

13

tive nets is a particularly useful frame of reference for understanding Sino-American communication.

Protection and Paranoia

All too often, when Chinese hosts cast a protective net "in friendship," Americans try to free themselves from it;[3] and when American hosts extend a hand in greeting, with little or no protective net attached, Chinese wonder about the sincerity of this "friendship" and even grow anxious about their sustained wellbeing.[4] Consequently, as any period of residence in China soon demonstrates, Chinese and Americans develop—along with mutual enjoyment and friendship—varying degrees of paranoia that can put even the most routine behavior under suspicion.

One explanation, of course, is that even paranoids have real enemies, as Henry Kissinger occasionally reminds us. China's governance involves both the overt system of public institutions with whose members we interact rather easily and the more shadowy system of political and security organs whose work usually is "not open" (*bugongkai*) yet imposes constraints on all manner of dealings with foreigners. A fundamental concern with national security and political rectitude both reflects and reinforces cultural resistance to alien influence; official Chinese

---

[3]At 4:30 a.m., a full hour before the end of an overnight train ride, I was helpfully awakened by the steward so that "you can wash your face." No one had told me to wash my face in almost forty years, and I rejected this solicitous concern out of hand!

[4]Many Americans were distressed in the early years of U.S.-PRC exchange to see Chinese delegations cordoned off by State Department security officers; how many realized that they represented *protection* fervently requested by the Chinese, not isolation imposed by the U.S. hosts? Women university students in China apologize for leaving their foreign roommate alone for a night because a Chinese friend's roommate will be away and needs their company; being alone is a frightening prospect.

14

"regulations" and "directives," both acknowledged and denied, form a backdrop to apparently spontaneous behavior. Chinese students and teachers *are* periodically reminded to deal with foreign residents only with caution, if at all. There *are* signs near every Chinese city reading "foreigners not permitted beyond this point," just as there are research facilities and industries in the U.S. that PRC Chinese (and others from socialist states) cannot freely visit. Telephonic eavesdropping is not an unknown practice in either country. The assumption of foreigners resident in China that their mail is regularly reviewed is probably fair enough in many cases, and Chinese scholars in the U.S. are hardly oblivious to the occasional invigilation of our government. While it is unlikely that, as one student in China claimed, "we Americans are constantly being followed," it would be naive to argue that such incidents never happen.

Despite the ubiquitous registration (*dengji*) system for Chinese entering foreigners' hotels and dormitories, Americans generally are quite innocent about the possible risks they pose to their Chinese friends and associates and are immensely distressed when confronted with them. But few Chinese, including those who seem most relaxed and straightforward, ever lose sight of the potential hazards or the extent to which they are "protected" in their associations with us. There are just enough "real" problems and constraints to keep a true paranoid of either nationality quite content, often to the great embarrassment of hosts in China and the U.S. who themselves have no wish or reason to express anything other than gracious hospitality.

A second element breeding suspicion is our inadequate understanding of the interactions among Chinese themselves. Like most foreigners, Americans are remarkably quick to see Chinese behavior as aimed specially at them, when in fact they simply are sharing in local culture. How many of us realize that the offensive "registration" of our Chinese guests is only an

15

extension of the system to which *everyone* normally is subjected when visiting Chinese offices? We are eager for home hospitality, to see how our friends and acquaintances "really live"; yet entertainment almost invariably is provided formally, in clubs or restaurants. We satisfy ourselves with the explanation that Chinese living quarters are small, humble and thus probably embarrassing to our potential hosts. While the explanation is usually true, it does not touch the heart of the matter: that home hospitality is rare among the Chinese and usually reserved for the very closest of friends and most special of occasions. One American teacher in China recently was astounded to learn from a Chinese woman who accepted her invitation that it was the first time in twenty years her guest had dined at a colleague's home. Similarly: why, despite endless visits to institutions and agencies, do we see only comfortable reception halls and common rooms, and never the offices of working staff? Why do foreign experts, hired by a Chinese institution, spend the bulk of their time in their hotel and feel so isolated from the hum of academic life? Perhaps because only the most senior Chinese professors and administrators have their own offices, while faculty members normally work at home, coming in only one or two days a week to lecture. We don't see the "work place" because so often there isn't any.

Given this context for communicating across cultures, even the purest motives and most gracious practices can yield ambiguous interpretations. The need to decipher the codes of "hospitality," "protection" and "interference" could be the largest single challenge in our cultural interactions. In this respect, the directness and informality of most Americans give our Chinese counterparts a great advantage in reading our intentions. We tend to do for others only what we would do for ourselves (with a little gilding, perhaps) and, after initial courtesy, quickly "tell it like it is." More than one Chinese friend has commented that their early post-Ping-Pong delegations were sometimes upset that U.S. hosts simply "dumped them at the hotel" in the evening, with no formal dinner or entertainment planned; but as this normal pattern of American hospitality became clear, along with our presumption that even honored guests are self-reliant adults, the sense of affront diminished rather quickly.

Americans, however, have a much harder time fathoming the meanings of China's double-edged hospitality. When barriers arise within an otherwise warm reception and our seemingly reasonable requests are blocked, *our* gorge also rises, for a variety of reasons: a) eager to learn and explore, we assume a right to learn more about Chinese society than we know even about our own (I, for one, haven't visited a U.S. farm, factory or courtroom since I left grammar school); b) few of us comprehend how basic and hence embarrassing are the Chinese standards of material life we yearn to sample; c) few Chinese will voluntarily explain the likely difficulties of such sampling, especially if the reasons might seem unpleasant; and d) the Chinese sense of personal responsibility for a guest's welfare is stronger than we can fully grasp. Repeated urgings that visitors be chauffeured even short distances have yielded the most sinister interpretations, since the common statement that "you might get lost" seems patently ridiculous. A direct (and honest) explanation that there *is* crime in the city, that traffic *can* be extremely hazardous, and that the "responsible persons" *could* be severely criticized if anything untoward happened is usually avoided, leaving Americans to read between the lines, often erroneously.

Meals in special restaurants and dining rooms become a symbol of the wish to isolate us from the people, from Chinese reality. A simple explanation that "people's" restaurants are crowded beyond our probable tolerance, dirty by Western standards, and serve generally unpalatable food would be painful in the giving, though not as painful as the humiliation of letting honored guests be so badly served or be the objects of public curiosity. But we then suspect that our Chinese hosts intend to shield us from learning about their society. Is all this generous hospitality meant simply to divert our attention from those other things we really want to do? (One wonders whether our Chinese guests believe that ordinary Americans really do stay in the air-conditioned opulence of a Hyatt, a Hilton or even a Holiday Inn; maybe we're just separating them from the people, or trying to deceive them about our affluence!)

The Pollyanna Syndrome

These unhappy suspicions usually develop only *after* real contact has begun—after we're actually caught up in China's protective net or after the Chinese are actually in the U.S. looking for one. They become salient largely because both sides have been so predisposed to think the very best, to make each other's virtues larger than life. "Marco Polo-itis" was defined long ago by Jerome Cohen as a disease of the American China traveller involving "paralysis of the critical faculties," an affliction that made us susceptible to the most benign interpretations of Cultural Revolution depravities and accepting of the monstrous deceptions they produced. Although the earlier epidemic has subsided, the disease has not been eradicated. Conversely, for Americans meeting Chinese young people today, it is hard to miss their underlying hope that our social problems and "spiritual crises" are not as serious as the media make out: that American ingenuity, science and even power really can be part of China's, and perhaps their personal salvation. With mutual expectations so high, reality easily becomes suspect.

One reflection of these Pollyanna tendencies is the familiar pattern of "out-politeing" each other, the fear of offending that so often shields both parties from candid talk and brass tacks. The euphoria of a lively dinner or warm discussion yields next morning to a realization that nothing much was learned or accomplished. The excessive courtesy—Chinese in origin and so attractive to us—is *not* uniformly apparent among Chinese themselves, and foreigners resident in China are often shocked by the pervasive "rudeness." The eagerly helpful, friendly, courteous and kind responses of friends and service personnel can quickly be eclipsed by the sullen indifference of people encountered in less personal settings. But courtesy usually is offered so compellingly to "foreign friends" that we actually can end up wildly misinformed. A minor example:

> A distinguished Chinese scholar, familiar both with English and with the West, uses the traditional term *taitai* in refer-ring to his wife, instead of the current *airen* (loved one). The Western interlocutor makes a mental note that the presumed demise of this "feudal" term is not complete, adding to his store of data for an article. Later, in another context, he mentions this apparent linguistic throwback and asks the scholar if its use is peculiar to this region. Answer: "Oh, no, we never use *taitai*. I used it only for you, since I didn't know if you were familiar with our new terminology!"

Caught up in a gracious reception, Americans new to China frequently find it difficult to press a line of questioning or to probe issues being dealt with circumspectly by their hosts. Appearing to doubt or question what one is told seems simply rude in the prevailing atmosphere. Yet this serves only to reinforce problems of communication. Within Chinese conversational style is a tendency to respond in terms of expectations, goals, even models rather than with mundane facts. Courtesy prompts *good* answers, not just technically accurate ones, and one strains to assume that what *should* be, *is,* or at least soon will be. Question: "Will your university have a Chinese language program for foreign students

19

this summer?'' Answer: ''Yes.'' ''How many students will you have?'' ''One hundred.'' But further questioning reveals that the institution simply has decided in *principle* to have a course, that no dates have been set, no students have yet applied, and no arrangements with foreign institutions made. For purposes of the question, however, a plan had become a concrete reality.

American scholars visiting China for a few weeks ask repeatedly about birth rates in the localities they visit and are impressed by the apparent success of population control efforts that the accumulated answers suggest. Only by accident toward the end of their stay do they realize that, in most cases, the figures given them were the *targets* for last year and this. Actual data had not yet been compiled, but the presumption of correspondence between goals and reality was strong enough to justify using the target figures. Probably not a conscious attempt to deceive, but a form of deception nevertheless to which the reluctance of foreign guests to probe too deeply made them accomplices. Yet, when persistence finally does uncover the ''truth,'' our suspicions are heightened, not allayed. Why aren't we given a ''straight answer'' in the first place?

Communication and Concepts

Our problems of mutual comprehension stem not only from cultural norms, but from more particular traits of thought and communication. The indirection that permeates Chinese speech, even in English translation, can be particularly disconcerting to Americans. ''Perhaps'' and ''maybe'' are cultural stock-in-trade. ''Maybe I will come with you'' usually means ''I'm coming.'' ''Perhaps it is too far for you to walk'' means ''There's no way I'll let you walk.'' When something is ''inconvenient,'' it most likely is impossible. But more than verbal indirection is at work here. The absence of a categorical statement implies that ''perhaps'' some room for discussion remains; and, in any case, a subsequent reversal will not represent a clear backing-down. Despite the firm signal that conditional speech often implies, negotiation is never totally foreclosed and dignity is maintained, at the expense of American patience.

When asked a seemingly "strange" question, Chinese tend helpfully to answer the one that *should* have been asked, but only that question, without trying to divine the real intent or volunteering more; thus they can appear entirely unhelpful. After finding a Chinese cable office dark early one evening, despite the sign giving its hours as 8:00-22:00, a visitor discovers two staffers in a back room inhaling their evening noodles. Question: "Is your office open?" Answer: "We're eating supper." "Ah, yes, I see that, but when will you be open?" Answer: "When we've finished supper." "But when will that be?" Answer: "Don't know, but not too long." "Well, is it likely to be before 6:00 p.m.?" Answer: "Yes, probably, please come back then." Given the rhythms of Chinese life, the original question should have been "When will you finish supper," and it should not have anticipated a precise response. Except for the cheerfulness of the replies, one could readily have assumed that these Chinese workers were more committed to secrecy or dissembling than to "serving the people." But it was simply a different style at work, one that places little value on volunteering information not specifically required to cope with the immediate issue at hand.

Phrases that Western visitors and residents in China must learn to live with are "we'll consider it" (*kaolu*) and "we'll study it" (*yanjiu*). These common responses to requests seem the ultimate in hedging and avoiding potentially difficult issues. But they also reflect the pervasive need in China to consult with higher-level colleagues before making decisions. Forgetting the foibles of our own bureaucratism, and unaware that routine tasks of communication at home can be major chores in the PRC, Americans quickly become frustrated by the need to consider-

21

and-study even the apparently simplest appeals.[5] We are dealing here with the way the *system* works, not only with verbal styles; but the difference is often hard to discern in our discourse with Chinese culture.

Other aspects of China's style also challenge our comprehension and patience. The sense of time, for example. Not until one has tried for several hours to dial a phone number before getting through, or in despair has taken a cab three miles to deliver the message, can one "know" what it means for things to take *time*. One phone (if any) per office, very few private lines, whole apartment buildings with one or two communal phones where messages can be left *if* someone answers. If one knows the informal network—who works or lives near whom and can serve as an intermediary—then things go faster; but it takes still more time to learn each informal network. Perhaps as a result, Chinese don't seem comfortable doing business by telephone, which for them is essentially a vehicle for communicating information or arranging future face-to-face sessions, not for discussing or resolving problems. Not so, of course, among friends and colleagues, but (relative to the U.S.) certainly true in conducting business across bureaucratic lines. Coordinating multi-office activities seems to be a major challenge to the norms of communication and the limited facilities that support them; how easily we forget our singular dependence on computers and copy machines at home. The effort of writing letters to foreigners, with all the approvals, translations and mechanics of typing on the few available machines (whether Chinese or English) that

---

[5] I recall the excitement and relief of being received in one major city by an unusually lively and direct woman guide for whom no request seemed too difficult. Her response to any question was "*Wenti buda!*" ("No big problem"), and arrangements were effortlessly made. Perhaps it was just that our requests were, in fact, relatively simple, but our three days without hearing "*kaolu, yanjiu*" were a joy.

this involves, merits a whole separate essay. The frustrations Americans feel in the absence of full and complete replies to our inquiries arise so often because we assume China's patterns of communication are like our own. Yet we can hardly expect an entire cultural system to revise its sense of time and process just because we enter it.

Although these aspects of communication are disconcerting to Americans, the basic modes of Chinese thought can be even more confusing. An excellent discussion of the "functionality" of Chinese ideas, particularly about education and study, comes in David Bonavia's recent book, *The Chinese*. It takes little time in China to witness this phenomenon and its bearing on "mutual understanding." If the purpose of study is "to make a contribution," to "learn something useful," as the Chinese believe it is, then what was I studying in China? "I'm studying China's education system." Derisive laughter! "What can you possibly learn from us? Our education system is a mess!" The idea that someone might seek to learn *about* China, not necessarily *from* China, seemed quite incomprehensible. An American wanting to pursue research on, say, China's agricultural credit, family planning or school curricula must be seeking useful information—not just a chance to fiddle with theoretical constructs. Hence, if Chinese hosts believe their programs are not in good shape and worthy of emulation, then we are either making a foolish request that doesn't merit serious attention or we're hiding our real motives.

Problems of comprehension are compounded by the common American personality that delights in action, in "making things happen," and in the private ego-satisfaction that results even without monetary or institutional rewards. We often create projects, offer assistance, or propose cooperation in large part because "we get a kick out of it." In response, our Chinese associates, more practically-minded, wonder what we're really after—what we have left unsaid. Their concern has roots in the history of American philanthropy in China and Chinese presumptions that our recently renewed "friendship" implies practical benefits. Surely our *intentions* are to help China, but since our motivation is often simply self-interest, suspicion can be the eventual outcome, for understandable reasons on both sides.

If the first Chinese priority is to learn the useful, the way to do it is not primarily by inductive analysis, but by emulation, by studying the successful experience of others. The PRC has made maximum use of this traditional approach; designation of model communes, model factories, model teachers, model workers has been paramount in the official reward system, and "Learn From . . ." campaigns are continually employed for pedagogy and political mobilization alike. While hardly alien to us, the reliance on "models" in China's civic life seems to the average Western visitor greatly overdone, rather like an adult Boy Scout camp or Sunday school. And it can involve direct consequences for us. One American student at a large Chinese university didn't know whether to laugh or cry when he discovered that several weeks previously he had been chosen "model foreigner"; the institution's Foreign Affairs Office had advised everyone in his department to observe him, to emulate his diligence and to learn from his example how a foreigner ought to behave in Chinese society. (After his discovery, he decided to sloppy-up a bit, just to clear his good name with his Western friends; he also surmised that some *negative* models must also have been selected among his peers!)

Innumerable writers and foreign visitors have noted the concern with "face" and "respect" that pervades Chinese culture. This concern may well be the glue that has held this ancient civilization together, reflecting the primacy of human relations (or "human feelings"—*renqing*) in Chinese values. It

24

would not normally occur to Americans to include in the text of solemn international treaties, academic exchange agreements or dinnertime toasts a vow to "respect" the other party. Yet it is commonplace in our dealings with Chinese, and we seem to relish it, both because it is China's equivalent of apple pie and motherhood and because we rather admire this virtue so often obscured at home. But this call for "respect" can be a cultural trap for Americans. One often *insists* on respect when its loss is feared, when the grounds for deserving it are either weak or unlikely to be understood. Chinese needs for respect often appear as defense mechanisms against possible criticism of conditions they believe we might *not* respect in our own society. A preemptive assurance of mutual respect is a superb diplomatic asset when foreigners later violate "Chinese customs" by taking "inappropriate" photographs, breaking the extremely early curfews in college dorms, visiting apparently innocuous places that technically are "not open," or expressing complaints so candidly as to cause embarrassment to a Chinese host. If the salience of "respect" in Chinese culture is admirable, it is also a mine-field for Americans not familiar with the insecurities underlying it and the diverse circumstances in which it can be invoked.

On Being Alien

One could write endlessly (as others have) about the characteristics of Chinese culture and behavior, and their differences with the West. But our concern here is the aggregate consequences for our interactions: namely, a profound sense among most Chinese that we are, indeed, alien. Our not being Chinese justifies intense curiosity about us, the most special treatment and, of course, selective emulation. Few if any long-term foreign residents of China, despite their acculturation and abiding love of the country, admit to being fully accepted, to being considered "non-foreign." There is great import in the old and probably true story of the missionary who, in good local dialect, asks a Chinese peasant directions to the next village. Getting only stoney silence, he walks away, only to overhear the peasant say to his friend, "Funny, it almost sounded like he was asking how to get to the next village." Having once assumed the tale apocryphal (though instructive), I learned better recently when driving along the Fujian coast and stopping in a small town to take a photo. It was only seconds before the inevitable mob of faces gathered to affix the dispassionate stares that all foreigners must live with. Trying as usual to unfreeze the tableau, I offered the front row some friendly wisecracks in Chinese, producing the equally usual smiles and *bonhommie*. Turning to snap the picture that was my purpose, I heard the middle-aged man at my left ear solemnly assure the group, "No, he's not a foreigner; he speaks Chinese!" Though I might have felt honored by this instant admission to Chinese civilization (perhaps as a Uighur from Xinjiang?), his logic clearly was different; nothing could be foreign and Chinese at the same time. Seeming in one respect Chinese, I could not possibly also be foreign. An either-or, black-and-white proposition that allows little room for degrees of acculturation or diversity.

Although this psychic distance is well reflected in the special tourist amenities noted earlier, it is most clearly expressed in the new foreigner "clubs," cocktail lounges (replete with pop-bands) and game rooms featuring pinball and Space Invader machines now appearing in China's major hotels. Both the thoughtfulness and commercial good sense of making foreigners feel at home can be appreciated; but the reproduction of our presumed natural habitat within an environment so extremely dissimilar is jarring—especially considering how little effort seems devoted to assuring either our easy access to *Chinese* social institutions or Chinese access to our special enclaves within the PRC.

Above and beyond the linguistic and cultural barriers to the latter course, the sharp separation of East and West seems more natural and instinctive to Chinese hosts than do imaginative efforts to blur the boundaries and encourage genuinely relaxed interchange. In this respect, cultural preferences, economic realities and official policy are mutually supportive—despite the irony that China is now busily replicating the "foreign concessions" that were a primary target of its Revolution.

In the end, it seems, the most supportive and protective net that China knows how to provide in her own land is the one that permits foreigners to live separate if not equal, to be treated very well but from a distance. Like the wider Chinese society it reflects, this pattern is not likely to change in a big hurry. Americans and Chinese will continue to communicate, face to face, across a cultural gap of sizeable proportions. Perhaps that is what makes real communication, when it does occur, so very rewarding.

The Chinese Language: Myths and Facts

TIMOTHY LIGHT

Few things in Chinese culture are more widely misunderstood outside of China than the Chinese language. The Chinese write very differently from us and indeed from all other literate societies in today's world except for Japan and Korea (which continue to make partial use of writing borrowed from China long ago). Even to the untutored eye, Chinese characters are not an alphabet, though many Americans who want to ask about them do not know what term to use for them, and questions are often asked such as, "Is it true that the Chinese alphabet . . . well, writing . . . I mean pictures, well . . . you know what I mean . . . they're very pictorial, aren't they?"

Because of the obvious radical difference between the way that the Chinese write and the way we write, many myths have grown up, not just around China's writing system, but around its language as a whole and around China's people. Indeed, people often say that the Chinese write in pictures. Many believe that Chinese is a monosyllabic language, which presumably means that every word in Chinese consists of a single syllable, like the English words *but, aim, quick, work, crime, laugh,* and unlike the words *although, goal, rapid, employment, transgression, guffaw.* Many believe that, because they write similarly (in part), Japanese, Korean and Chinese people are related. Many assume that because of their language, the Chinese think in a way that is radically different from our way of thinking. Regarding modern Chinese, a common myth holds that the Communist government has done away with Chinese characters and has substituted a brand new alphabet that all people now use instead of characters. It is further believed that this supposed change has been tantamount to abandonment of the Chinese language itself. In addition, some believe that the Communist government has wiped out the various Chinese dialects.

Each of these beliefs and assumptions is false. Each of them is in its own way outrageous, since taken together they suggest that the capacity for language among the world's largest national-ethnic group is somehow different from that of all other human groups, a suggestion for which there is no evidence. To examine thoroughly these unhelpful myths would require greater scope than this short essay will permit. But in the following pages, I shall outline some basic facts about the Chinese language. In doing this, I shall try to correct the myths that I have just listed.

Chinese belongs to the Sino-Tibetan language group. Sino-Tibetan is a major genetic grouping of languages like the Indo-European family to which English belongs (along with German, French, Hindu, etc.). The Sino-Tibetan speech community stretches from Northeastern India to Northeastern China, and its billion-plus speakers are found in Southeast Asia, South Asia and East Asia. Chinese itself is not a single language, but a language family like the Romance language family to which French, Spanish, Italian, Romanian and Swiss Romansch belong. Like the Romance languages, the Chinese languages are mutually unintelligible (that is what makes them different languages). But, because they share a common history and a good deal of common vocabulary and grammar, it is much easier for a speaker of one Chinese language to learn another Chinese language than for a complete outsider to do so. Again, this is true of the Romance languages as well. The Chinese languages referred to here are the famous Chinese "dialects": Cantonese, Shanghai, Fukienese, etc. Because speakers of one of these "dialects" cannot understand speakers of another of them, the "dialects" are as much real languages as are the Romance languages.

There are two ways, however, in which the analogy to the Romance language family is inaccurate. Most of the Romance languages are identified with separate independent countries and bear a name related to their place of "origin." There is no such political identification of nation with language in China. Politically and ethnically, China has retained the ideal of unity for well over two millennia. Although at times China has been divided by external conquest and civil war, the divisions have never identified parts of China as separate nations, and the language groups of China have never been the rallying point for political or military separatism.

The other important difference between the Romance languages and Chinese lies in China's writing system. After the spread of Roman civilization during the expansionist years of the Roman Empire, Romance dialects grew to a position very much like that of the Chinese "dialects." Each region of the Roman world had a language that was Romance in origin and in vocabulary and grammar, but that had become incomprehensible to speakers of other Romance "dialects" through linguistic change and influence from the languages of the peoples who preceded the Romans in that area. Yet, although the languages of the various areas were so different, the written language was relatively uniform. That written language was, of course, Latin, the standard language of Rome. Latin retained its standard form for a very long time because of the prestige of Rome first as a political and then as a religious capital, and because of the low rate of literacy prevalent in pretechnical societies. Once Rome's power began to decline and the independence of the outlying areas increased, people more and more wrote as they spoke, using the symbols of the Roman alphabet to reflect their own pronunciations and way of forming words instead of those proper to Latin.

Reflecting speech is a natural thing for an alphabet to do, since alphabets are a phonetic way of writing. Because Chinese is *not* alphabetic, its writing does *not* reflect differences and changes in speech. Even though two speakers of different Chinese languages cannot understand each other (and thus may have to resort to a foreign language such as English for oral communication), they can write to each other and thereby understand each other. The ways that they read aloud what they have written will differ almost completely, but the meaning of what has been written will be identically clear to each. Written Chinese reflects the vocabulary and grammar of the most broadly used Chinese oral language. Speakers of the nonstandard Chinese languages learn this vocabulary and grammar, often pronouncing the words in their own local ways when they learn to read and write. In short, the written language of China is uniform despite China's actual language diversity and the mutual unintelligibility of the several Chinese languages.

The earliest origin of this writing system was in fact pictorial. These early characters dating from perhaps three thousand years ago illustrate how Chinese writing began:

(Blood)	(Sun,) Day	(Moon) Month	(Water)	(Heaven)	(Horse)

But this early start with pictorial writing was quickly abandoned. It is difficult for pictures to represent abstract thoughts, and different people's drawings of the same object may differ greatly. It is simply cumbersome to express lengthy messages by pictures. As writing became more common and as the nature of written material became more diverse, Chinese writing grew more and more stylized and less pictorial. In the third century B.C., Chinese writing was officially standardized to a form that is not too distant from today's Chinese writing. Since that time, the pictorial origins of Chinese writing have been largely obscured by the uniformity imposed on the writing to make it more efficient. Here are the same characters given above, but now in modern form.

(Blood)	(Sun, Day)	(Moon, Month)	(Water)	(Heaven)	(Horse)

The pictures are evident only to those who have been informed that pictures are present. Much more important than graphic representation in written symbols has been the combination of an element in a character that suggests the pronunciation at the time of the character's creation and the one that indicates something about the semantic category of the meaning (i.e., human, mechanical, liquid, insect, etc.). The following characters are made up of such combinations. In each of the four cases shown below, the category indicator lies to the left and the pronunciation indicator to the right.

(He)	(Machine)	(Juice)	(Mosquito)

33

Chinese characters in their modern form remain the only regular medium for writing standard Chinese in the world today. In the PRC, some of the most complex or frequently used characters have been simplified by reducing their number of "strokes," or lines, in order to make them easier to learn to read and write. Furthermore, some of the least frequently used characters have been merged into a single character. The reduction of strokes is exemplified in the following characters:

(Hear)   (10,000)   (Machine)

This simplification of the writing in China has been accompanied by a massive effort at literacy training and an intensive campaign to promote Mandarin, the standard dialect, as the national language. The results of these campaigns have been outstanding. China's literacy rate has risen from between twenty and thirty percent to between eighty and ninety percent, a remarkable achievement for a nation with one of the most difficult writing systems to learn. Along with the spread of literacy in China has gone the extension of the use of Mandarin as the national spoken language and the adoption of a standard spelling system called *pinyin* that uses the Roman alphabet to spell the pronunciation of Chinese characters. *Pinyin,* replacing a variety of older, unstandardized romanization systems, is used as a reference tool in dictionaries, as a supplement to characters on signs and titles, and as the means of introducing standard pronunciation of characters to primary school first graders. In 1979, China's news agency began using the *pinyin* spellings of names and places in dispatches, and Americans had to get used to Mao Zedong and

Zhou Enlai instead of the more familiar Mao Tse-tung and Chou En-lai. Some American newspapers mistakenly reported this adoption of the *pinyin* system as a decision to abandon characters for the alphabet. Although there are some in China who advocate such a move, and although such a change is contemplated by planners of very long-term policy, there is no likelihood of it occurring soon.

China has thus not followed the lead of Japan in reorganizing its writing system. Japanese writing incorporates both Chinese characters and symbols that have a sound value like an alphabet (called a syllabary). Because of their syllabary, the Japanese are able to learn much more quickly than the Chinese to write their language intelligibly, even if not elegantly. (Elegance and style require the use of characters in Japanese.) Japanese differs from Chinese not only in its writing, but in almost all other aspects as well. Along with Korean, Japanese is related to the Altaic language family, which includes Turkish but not Chinese. In Japanese there is a highly elaborated system of hierarchical expression for speaking with persons of different social levels, something Chinese does not have. In Japanese, verbs come at the end of a sentence; in Chinese they come in the middle. In Japanese, the characters may be read with words of several syllables. In Chinese, every character is read with a single syllable. To sum up, although the two languages both employ written characters, their differences outweigh their similarities, and Americans should not assume that the two languages have much in common.

Each Chinese character is pronounced as a single syllable. This is the source of the myth that Chinese is monosyllabic. The truth is that most Chinese words are polysyllabic and are written in clusters of characters. Most words in modern Chinese are two syllables (i.e. two characters). Thus, *ming* means "clear, bright" and is written with the character 明 , and *bai* means "white,

blank'' and is written 白. Put together, *mingbai* 明白 means
"understand, clear,'' and only *mingbai* can be used to mean
"understand.'' *Ming* can never be used alone, and *bai* means
something different when it is used alone.

The most troublesome myth to deal with is the one which
maintains that, because their language is structured differently
from ours, the Chinese necessarily think differently from
Westerners. One of the silliest versions of this myth that I have
heard is the claim that science cannot be practiced in Chinese
because that language is not "scientific." (Since all languages
are about equal in their inconsistencies and irregularities, it is
difficult to know what the word "scientific" means when applied
to a language.)

The idea that Chinese and Westerners think differently
because of linguistic differences is, in my opinion, unconvincing.
Indeed I find very little hard evidence to prove that language
and thought are intertwined in any culture. Certainly, our
individual thoughts and the specific language in which we express
them are inseparable. But that does not mean that what we say
in our own language may not have direct equivalents in another
language if what we say happens to be spoken by someone with
our same aims.

The only serious attempt that I am familiar with to show
that language and thought are causally related has been made
in comparatively technical statements such as the speculation
that in Eskimo languages doing physics may be difficult because
there is no linguistic reference for past, present and future time.
The only such technical statement of any plausibility seriously
proposed by a noted scholar of Chinese (in this case, by the
eminent Sinologist, L.S. Yang) is the speculation that classical
Chinese may not express the notion, so basic to logic, of "the
principle of the excluded middle." That principle holds that with
reference to any other quality, any phenomenon can be said

exclusively to belong to the quality or not (or, put more simply, a phenomenon can't *be* something and *not be* it at the same time). For example, a classical Chinese statement such as, ''The horse is not a vegetable'' may have been less absolute in its negation than it sounds; that is, it may have left room for vagueness. Even if this should turn out to be true, it does not mean that speakers of classical Chinese could not understand the notion of exclusivity or that they did not in fact use this notion in their reasoning. Certainly this does not suggest at all that the Chinese ever confused horses and cabbages.

Other, less plausible assertions about the way that the Chinese language makes the Chinese people think include these: the Chinese do not distinguish between one and many because their words are not marked for singular and plural; the Chinese do not know the difference between definite and indefinite because their language lacks articles; the Chinese do not always understand the differences between past, present and future because their verbs are marked for change and completion rather than directly for time reference; the Chinese do not clearly understand the difference between counterfactual statements and possible ones (e.g. ''If I were you, I would . . . '' vs. ''If I go, I will . . . '') because their language does not have any *formal* ways to distinguish the two. If any of these assertions were true, it is unlikely that the Chinese race would have survived three or four millennia, since the Chinese would be always in the wrong place with the wrong objects and quite uncertain about whether they were there or not.

Most such misunderstandings come naturally from an inadequate understanding on the part of non-Chinese who are attempting to analyze Chinese. Some of it also comes from Chinese speakers who inadequately comprehend Western languages.

There is, however, one relationship between thought and

language which is not myth. That relationship is exemplified in Chinese by the tendency of ordinary Chinese to understate, or to convey meaning indirectly. Not only do the Chinese not share our predilection for expletives of a superlative intent such as "Terrific!" "Great!" "Fantastic!" and the like, but they frequently describe situations through understatement, double negatives, apparent vagueness, euphemism and allusive language. In negotiation, an agreement to a proposal may be given as *wenti buda* which literally means "The problems are not great." This tendency is related to formulaic expressions in Chinese such as *bucuo* "no error" = "right you are," *bushao* "not few" = "a lot," *chabuduo* "off not much" = "approximately." Similarly, a denial may take the form of "Perhaps it's not convenient" or "Possibly the time isn't right" when refusing to respond to a proposal that is seen as impossible to implement. Criticism is often given indirectly, but effectively. Frequently historical allusion is used to describe a situation that the critic does not like, and the reader or hearer is left to infer who in contemporary life is being castigated. The former head of state, Liu Shaoqi, was labelled as "China's Khruschev" in the months before he was publicly denounced and brought down. The late premier, Zhou Enlai, was identified with Confucius in the Anti-Confucius/Anti-Lin movement of the early seventies. Naturally, political labels and symbols form a major part of the vocabulary of both criticism and approbation, though it seems that the vocabulary for identifying deviants (right winger, right deviationist, capitalist roader, ultra-leftist, those who use the red flag to oppose the red flag, etc.) is much greater than that for identifying model citizens (as is equally true of the language use of the Christian Church).

It is important to realize that these usages are not new in Chinese society; only the specific terms, such as those with

Marxist-Leninist content, are new. The tendencies to indirectness and allusion are ancient cultural traits of the Chinese, and politicians and negotiators were using them as much hundreds of years ago as they are now. This use of language is an expression of a cultural preference for harmonious and positive intercourse among people. It is a cultural expression, not a control of thought by language. Language is simply one of the tools through which a society expresses its character, and it is to be expected, not wondered at, that Chinese society expresses the same characteristics through its languge as it does in other cultural forms.

Because the focus of American relations with China has moved within the past three or four years from diplomatic sorting out to business connections, there is one area of cultural expression in language that must be mentioned in closing. That concerns the use of a special language for legal purposes. In our society, legal language is so specialized that it alone often makes the difference between one party's satisfaction and the other's in a hotly contested dispute. Our legal profession is a huge body of technocrats trained principally in the wielding of the tool of legal language. It is often noted that China has a tiny number of lawyers (as does Japan) compared to the United States. This is not primarily because Chinese criminal proceedings have failed to allow sufficient protection for defendants (though that has often been true), but because binding relations involving the exchange of money, goods and services are not sealed in immutable language in China. Rather, contracts lay out basic wishes of both sides and fundamental intents; from our point of view, at least, a great deal is left to the common sense and mutual trust of the parties concerned. That procedure is unobjectionable so long as the expectations and assumptions of the two sides are the same. But troubles may arise when they differ. Different expectations, of course, are more likely to occur when the parties are from different cultures and when the principal participants do not know each other's language well.

China's joint-venture law of 1979 is a case in point. That law simply states general principles and does not contain the level of detail that American and other Western business executives would consider normal in their own societies. Because of the vagueness of the language used, many businesses hoping for deals in China have held back from entering joint ventures for fear of losing their investment should something not planned for occur.

Misunderstandings related to language—particularly those that lead to troublesome problems—come from cultural misperceptions and language incompetence, not from the different structures of the two languages that two peoples speak. So long as we in America remember that Chinese is one of the world's human languages and make intelligent provisions for the training of enough Americans in the use of that language, we face little problem from the uniqueness of the way that the Chinese speak and write. But if we continue our historical ignorance of both China's culture and its language, we doom ourselves to a very conflict-ridden relationship.

The Art of Interpreting

JAN CAROL BERRIS

Exchanges with the People's Republic of China have proliferated to a degree unimagined just a short time ago. As recently as 1977, fewer than twenty Chinese delegations visited the United States during the whole year; in 1982 delegations were averaging about 100 per month. This enormous increase in contact has necessitated a corresponding increase in the number of Chinese and Americans who can communicate in each other's language. Although many Chinese are learning English (it is by far the most important foreign language in China) and a few Americans know Chinese, interpreters are and will continue to be essential in facilitating communication between both sides.

Interpreting, as I have learned through more than a decade of experience, is a physically exhausting and often emotionally draining art. But those who work with interpreters can do a great deal to help maximize the interpreter's effectiveness and minimize his or her weaknesses.

What Makes a Good Interpreter?

Many people assume that anyone fluent in two languages can function as an interpreter. Indeed, a good command of both languages and alertness to their constant evolution is the foundation of effective interpreting. But that is only the first step. Expressing your own thoughts, choosing your own words and picking your own sentence patterns in a foreign tongue are very different—and infinitely easier—than precisely reproducing someone else's ideas, phrases and nuances. At the National Committee on U.S.-China Relations, we interview many people with Chinese language skills ranging from fairly good to excellent. Yet in an interpreting test, nearly all, even those who do quite well in general conversation, fall apart.

A good interpreter is more than a translator of words, since language skills are only a part of the process of communication. Biculturalism—sensitivity to cultural and social differences—is often as important as bilingualism. An interpreter must be sensitive to what is appropriate to the occasion. One of my favorite examples of this concerns a famous Western scientist who was asked to address a large Chinese audience. Before his talk, he was disconcerted to find that a number of children were playing and chattering in the aisles. His impatience increased when he realized that no one was attempting to quiet them down as he was about to begin. He exploded angrily at the interpreter, "Will you tell those little bastards to shut up!" With perfect aplomb the interpreter spoke quietly into the microphone, "Xiao pengyoumen, qing nimen shaowei anjing yidian, hao bu hao!" Which roughly translates, "Little friends, would you please be just a bit more quiet, if you don't mind."

Another important aspect of biculturalism is knowing what

makes people laugh in the other culture. Humor is very difficult to translate. In fact, very often American humor just does not work in Chinese. In that case one may have to resort to the tactic of Doonesbury's interpreter Honey (who is actually modeled on one of China's best interpreters, Tang Wensheng) when she tells her audience in one frame, ''I think he's about to make a joke . . . .'' and in the next, ''The joke has been made, and he will be expecting you to laugh at it. Go wild.''

Political sensitivity is also an essential aspect of biculturalism. Several times during the past decade we have been spared unhappy incidents when interpreters wisely avoided repeating an American speaker's inadvertent use of ''Republic of China'' for ''People's Republic of China'' and translated the latter term into Chinese. No matter how often people are forewarned about this error it is still quite common, whether out of nervousness or habit—especially when one is attempting a phrase like, ''the people of the People's Republic of China.'' Somehow that mouthful usually comes out wrong.

Bilingualism and biculturalism can be learned—though often only by a process of osmosis—during long years of study and/or living in another country. But there are other, more innate characteristics that contribute to the making of a good interpreter.

Good interpreters must have a special kind of personality, in fact, a somewhat schizophrenic one. On the one hand, they must be confident and aggressive enough to be relaxed when speaking in front of audiences large or small, presidents or prime ministers. On the other hand, they must have the ability to submerge their own egos and take on the personalities of the speakers. Frustrated actors probably make some of the best interpreters. They don't mind, in fact they enjoy, mirroring the actions and tones of the speaker or, as is quite often the case, a series of speakers with varying demeanors. Yet sometimes an interpreter can be too much of a ham. This is dangerous because while it makes for an entertaining, lively session, it usually detracts from the speaker, who should be the focus of attention.

Another theatrical talent that comes in handy is projection. Occasionally interpreters have the use of a microphone; more often they have to compete against the whir and rumble of factory machinery or city street noises. Some interpreters have a tendency to look at and speak directly to the leader of a delegation, ignoring the rest of the group. Many times I have found myself in the back of a room, waving my arms or otherwise trying to indicate to the interpreter that the people at the back cannot hear.

These personal traits often compensate for minor language problems. For instance, one interpreter with whom we have worked over the years speaks excellent Chinese, but in a classical, literary style. As an academic interested in traditional China he has not needed to be conversant with contemporary language changes. But since this particular person is also a consummate actor with exaggerated movements and facial expressions, we overlook his literary rather than vernacular language. Although he sometimes interjects too much of himself into the interpreting process, we also like to work with him because he interacts very well with the Chinese. They have great respect for his knowledge of traditional China, and they love to imitate (with great affection) his mannerisms and speech patterns.

On a more practical note, being able to do two (or more) things at one time is important. An interpreter must be listening to what the speaker is saying while thinking about the best way to render it into another language. This is obviously much more critical for simultaneous interpreters, but those who do consecutive interpreting face the problem as well. A few interpreters manage to do four things at the same time: listen; jot down key words to jog their memories; look up unknown words in a small dictionary (which usually appears magically out of a pocket); and, juggling notebook and dictionary, write down the unfamiliar word so if it is repeated later the dictionary will not have to be hauled out again. All this without diverting attention from the speaker.

And speaking of writing things down, interpreters should always carry notebooks—and use them. Even the best of memories sometimes fails. But one should be selective. Only those with super stenographic skills should attempt a verbatim transcript; otherwise they will still be on the third word while the speaker is waiting for the translation. Selected words or phrases should be sufficient to recall the full sentence.

Obviously interpreters should be matched to specific jobs; some will be better at one kind of work while others will excel at another. For technical interpreting someone who not only knows the specific jargon (that, after all, can be looked up in a dictionary) but also is familiar with the concepts behind the words is needed.

There are times when an interpreter who blends into the background is required, perhaps for high-level diplomatic negotiations. At other times, someone with a more forceful personality is required. The National Committee on U.S.-China Relations opts for the latter, since our work generally entails introducing Chinese and American counterparts to one another. Our interpreters must be observant, outgoing and interested in others, so that in a social situation they can get a group of Americans to stop chatting with their friends and encourage them to interact with the Chinese who, more than likely, have clustered themselves in the corner or at a window to exclaim over the view. We also need interpreters who are lively and knowledgeable about the United States so they can help explain American culture and history to members of Chinese delegations.

Background and Training of Interpreters

The interpreters whom Americans rely on, whether in China or in the United States, are either Americans for whom Chinese is not a native tongue (referred to below as "Americans"), citizens of the PRC or Chinese-Americans. Each has a distinctive background, and while it is impossible to predict on the basis of the background how interpreters will perform, a brief description of the three types may be useful.

Americans. Most American interpreters probably began with courses in Chinese language, history, politics, economics and society at universities in the United States. Following this initial training, the majority had an intensive language and cultural experience that solidified their foundation, broadened their vocabulary and exposed them to the problems of communicating with Chinese people.

Before 1979, this intensive experience usually took place in Taiwan (though individuals who have taken all four summers of the Middlebury College program, the U.S. Foreign Service course or perhaps the Army program at Monterey have become successful interpreters). Since 1979, the number of people who have lived for a year or two in China and come back with good language and cross-cultural knowledge has increased. Some have studied Chinese formally at a Chinese university or at one of the language institutes in Beijing. Others have learned or improved their Chinese in the process of teaching, working or conducting research. Many from this group make excellent interpreters. They have developed a strong vocabulary, ease of expression and effective personal relations. But it should not be assumed that a year or two of working or studying in China automatically produces a good interpreter.

Chinese language study in the United States and Taiwan has not caught up with the evolution of vocabulary on the

46

mainland, but this does not usually hamper a good interpreter. The differences are easily learned, especially by those sensitive to the political distinctions. In fact, a Taiwan background can be an advantage for an interpreter assisting a PRC delegation, since its members are often quite curious about conditions on the island.

Citizens of the PRC. Chinese in the PRC become interpreters primarily because of their language skills. English is now taught in China as early as the third grade, and students who excel are sent, after high school graduation, to a foreign language institute for advanced training. In addition, government agencies that have a foreign mission (the foreign ministry, the foreign trade apparatus, the military, etc.) have set up their own programs to insure that their interpreters will have the requisite technical skills. Many of the older English-language interpreters began as Russian interpreters and then switched fields in the early 1960s as Sino-Soviet relations deteriorated.

Up until 1979, most of the teachers at foreign language institutes were Chinese, though there were some foreign instructors. That has changed somewhat in the last two or three years. There are now 1,200 Americans living in China, the majority of whom are teachers working in major cities. As a result, the Chinese are learning American-English not British-English, as was the case before. Moreover, access to spoken English is now greater, due to Voice of America, the English language classes that are broadcast several times daily on radio and television and the increased number of Americans visiting China. As with American interpreters, however, there is no substitute for experience in an English-speaking country. Of the top ten Chinese interpreters that I know, in terms of both bilingualism and biculturalism, only two have not lived either in England, Canada, or the U.S. Repeated trips abroad, accompanying Chinese delegations, also strengthens an interpreter's skills.

Chinese-Americans.   Clearly, ethnic Chinese who have spent a number of years in the United States are another pool of potential interpreters. The great majority grew up speaking Chinese and absorbing Chinese cultural and social values and can be of enormous help in sensitizing Americans to potential or actual problems. Indeed, some of the National Committee's best interpreters are Chinese-Americans. But it is a fallacy to assume automatically that a Chinese-American will make a good interpreter. The decandants of Chinese who came to the U.S. before the Second World War probably speak a South China dialect rather than *putonghua* (the standard national dialect), if they speak Chinese at all. Their knowledge of the PRC may be minimal. Some of those who have come to the U.S. more recently, either from Taiwan or the PRC, may, for understandable political reasons, find it difficult to work with delegations from the People's Republic. Or the personal qualities mentioned before may be missing.

The Interpreting Situation

Even if competent interpreters are available, many communication problems can still occur. Insuring that they do not is as much the responsibility of those relying on interpretation as it is of the interpreter. This is particularly true for an American who is conducting negotiations or substantive discussions with the Chinese and who has a clear stake in their success. But everyone involved should be aware of certain pitfalls and try to avoid them.

Many of the problems listed below can be alleviated with some advance planning. Others need to be handled on the spot. All require open and honest communication between the employer and the interpreters.

Number of interpreters.   Since interpreting can be tiring, it is clearly better to have at least two interpreters, so that one can rest while the other is working. The result will be interpreting of a higher quality. Of course this is not always feasible and, in fact, in business negotiations it may be preferable to have one interpreter for the sake of continuity and consistency. However, one or two interpreters will definitely not be enough to cover social situations—dinners, cocktail parties—where there are ten or fifteen non-English speaking Chinese. For that big a group one interpreter for every four or five Chinese is a sound rule. These interpreters need not be professionals. Often Chinese speakers in the community will be able to do a satisfactory job of translating informal social conversation.

Monitors.   If it is not possible to have more than one interpreter for formal sessions, it is extremely useful to use someone with reasonably good Chinese to monitor conversations to insure that all that has been said in one language is accurately translated into the other. A nearby university with a Chinese studies program is a good place to look for individuals who can fill this role. If two interpreters are available, it is a good idea to have one monitor while the other interprets. Whatever the arrangement, it is important that everyone involved understand the division of labor so that no one loses face.

Preparation.   It is always useful for the interpreter to have some advance knowledge of the material to be translated so that unfamiliar terms can be checked and unclear concepts defined. Providing the interpreter with a copy of the text, promotional brochures about the product that is going to be sold or information about the sites to be visited is always worth the effort. If written material isn't available or if the speaker prefers to talk off-the-cuff, it is a good idea for the speaker to go over the issues that will be addressed in the discussion with the interpreter beforehand.

Other duties.   Given the exhausting nature of interpreting, interpreters should not be given other responsibilities, except when absolutely necessary. It is certainly not fair to expect the interpreter, in addition to being responsible for the substance of a discussion, to worry about finding a doctor if someone is sick or tracking down lost baggage.

Pacing.   How long an interpreter can work without losing effectiveness depends very much on the individual. I know a number of Americans and Chinese who can go from 8:00 in the morning until 1:00 the next morning. On the other hand, there are some people who cannot concentrate for more than a two-hour span, and need regular breaks to recharge their batteries. Obviously, knowing the interpreter's capacity in advance is very useful in planning agendas. Once discussions begin, the person in charge should look for clues that the interpreter is tiring.

Precision vs. paraphrase.   The interpreter should always be given a sense of how precise a translation is expected. For an interpreter to stay up the whole night toiling over an exact, word-for-word translation of a speech is counterproductive if the occasion does not demand it.

Another aspect of this issue is when to translate and when to leave people alone. I am of the school that believes that it is better to over-translate than to under-translate. There are those who feel that it is not important to translate everything that is said, especially when the conversation is not a substantive or professional one or when there are visual aids. But I think that interpreters, because they are bilingual, often forget what it is like to be in a strange land with no knowledge whatsoever of the language or culture. The non-English-speaking Chinese do not know that the spiel being given by the trainer at Sea Life Park is not all that relevant. While it might not be necessary to go into great detail in such situations, a quick paraphrase would at least give the Chinese the gist and let them know that they are not missing something really important.

Sometimes we encounter interpreters who feel the need for great precision and will take several seconds (which always seem like eons to listeners) to think of the word or phrase carrying the precise nuance of the situation. This is very commendable and certainly necessary in delicate diplomatic or business negotiations. But for general interpreting, it is more important to keep the flow of speech constant and use the closest approximation so as not to have an awkward silence (during which the speaker is apt to feel compelled to start talking again, thereby throwing the interpreter off balance).

Another kind of interpreter is the paraphraser or editor who tends to give the gist of what the speaker is saying, ignoring the details. If such actions stem from the interpreter's laziness, fatigue or boredom, it is inexcusable. But if the interpreter "reads" the audience well enough to know that they are indeed tired or not interested, it is forgiveable and indeed often desirable to speed things up a bit by omissions or condensations. For instance, before White House and Congressional tours, the National Committee escorts always tell the guides that the Chinese are generally unfamiliar with names of European sculptors, painters and craftsmen, and with the minutiae of American history. Yet the guides cannot seem to stop themselves from cataloging who painted which portrait of a president's wife and which glass company in what year produced the goblets used by President Hayes! At such times we do not complain if the interpreters leave out some details.

In general, where one strikes a balance depends on the nature of the situation. Usually, only business or diplomatic negotiations demand a precise, word-for-word translation. In other situations, accuracy is the goal but it is permissible to paraphrase on occasion.

Supplying background information. Sometimes, trying to be

helpful and fill in gaps in the audience's understanding, interpreters will add background information not supplied by the speaker. This is often quite useful, but the interpreter should indicate to the speaker that this has been done, especially since the speaker may have planned to give the same explanation in the very next sentence.

Length of speech units. Most people are not used to working with interpreters and often talk in long, rambling sentences. Forgetting to pause for translation, they leave the interpreter to scribble madly in a notebook or else to cough discreetly or in some way break into the monologue. Chinese interpreters tend to be more patient and will stand diligently taking notes until the bitter end, perhaps because they are more carefully trained or less aggressive (or more respectful of authority?) than some of their American colleagues. Occasionally the opposite will occur. In an effort to be as helpful as possible, an American speaker will give a phrase at a time, stopping in the middle of sentences and thoughts to allow the interpreter to translate. This may work in some languages, but not in Chinese. Since subject, verb and object generally occupy different positions in many English and Chinese sentences, interpreters need to have nearly the whole sentence in hand before they set to work. Speakers should always be reminded of this problem.

Invisibility of interpreters. Quite a few interpreters tend to speak in the third rather than in the first person. If the speaker is a proud father and wants to regale the listener with stories about his son, the interpreter should say "my son" and should not say "he says his son . . . ."

Interpreters should confine themselves to facilitating communication, and not (except in unusual situations) add their own personal comments. This is a very difficult thing to do; it is even harder when an American looks directly at the interpreter and asks questions that are meant for the delegation member:

52

"What's the next stop on the itinerary?" "How many children do you have?" "What has impressed you most about the United States?" The interpreter knows very well that the next stop is San Francisco, that the delegation member has three children aged 28, 24, and 18 (and even what they all do), and has heard twenty times how impressed the Chinese are with the warmth and friendliness and hospitality of Americans. But that knowledge is no excuse for not turning to the Chinese and asking once again, thus drawing the Chinese into the conversation.

Direction of translation. It is always easier to interpret into one's native tongue from the foreign language. Diplomatic practice, however, has made the opposite the rule, based on the theory that as part of a negotiating team, an interpreter is familiar with his or her own side's position and is able to render it better than someone unfamiliar with the background. Thus when interpreters are available from both sides, it is common for American interpreters to go from English to Chinese and for Chinese interpreters to work from Chinese to English even though articulateness would be increased if this were reversed.

Numbers. Even the best Chinese and American interpreters have problems with large numbers, since the Chinese arrange digits in sets of four, as opposed to sets of three in the West. Numbers should always be checked, especially if the translation seems surprising. Writing figures down and asking the interpreter whether they are correct is the best way of guaranteeing that one hundred thousand has not become one million.

Translating substance. It is inevitable that Americans will think and talk in their own categories, which do not necessarily have an analogue in Chinese. This can create problems, especially when the interpreter translates rather mechanistically. One way to compensate is for the Americans to learn as much as possible about China, so that they are more likely to use concepts that Chinese can understand, and, in turn, be able to better comprehend Chinese concepts.

Another dimension of this problem is the American tendency to express ideas in abstract and complex ways, while Chinese are accustomed to more concrete modes of expression. Providing a translation bridge over this gap can often prove very difficult, especially since there is no subjunctive mode in Chinese.

Questions.   The above difference is particularly evident when it comes to questions. Americans often preface questions with statements and then pose their queries in a theoretical fashion. Chinese are more used to questions that are direct, down-to-earth and pragmatic. Straight-forward rather than hypothetical questions will produce better results.

Chinese, especially officials, like to listen to a whole series of questions before giving any answers. They are masters at taking eighteen different questions and then weaving one statement that conveys their message, answers those queries they wish to address and barely touches those they wish to avoid. Americans can escape this trap by suggesting a question-by-question approach, on the grounds that the answer to one question will spark new and more interesting questions.

Non-verbal communication.   There are two ways in which body language can affect interpreter-aided communication. The first is in choosing whom one looks at. Most people tend to look at the interpreter when they really should look at the person being addressed. When listening to what is being interpreted one should try to look at the person who first said it. Doing this seems unnatural, and the Chinese are better at it than we are. Second, talking with your hands seems to aid communication. Listeners can pick up a vague idea of what it is being said even before the interpreter translates.

Helping with problems.   None of us is perfect—including interpreters. But weak points can be minimized. If the interpreter's problem is comprehension, speaking slowly will help.

If it is a vocabulary problem, having a good dictionary and paraphrasing creatively are partial remedies. Once when interpreting for a Chinese delegation, I totally blanked on how to say, "The sun set." So I just said, "The sun went to sleep." They got the idea and I got a lot of laughs! Above all, interpreters should receive frequent doses of positive reinforcement and, if necessary, constructive criticism.

Improving the Interpreting Profession

Unfortunately, the National Committee on U.S.-China Relations and other exchange organizations face a serious problem in holding on to good interpreters. It obviously takes great intelligence and skill to excel at this kind of work. Understandably, many interpreters with these qualities have ambitions that take them beyond interpreting. They want to be the ones giving rather than interpreting the speeches. It is also sad but true that the inadequate appreciation and compensation offered to interpreters dissuade some able people from entering the profession and induce many others to depart prematurely. This means that we must constantly look for new interpreters as ours move on to more psychologically or financially rewarding professions or, as is increasingly the case these days, go off to China for a year or so of study or work with a higher-paying corporation or translation service.

It is interesting to note that China has the same problem. Chinese who have spent time abroad and would therefore be good interpreters are not likely to take up the profession because it is not highly regarded. In fact, only a small fraction of the 8,000 PRC students in this country are studying to be interpreters. In spite of the cross-cultural sensitivity learned abroad, most will by choice go back and be scientists and engineers. Many people now working as interpreters look upon it as a stepping stone to something else. Thus many Chinese who were trained before 1949 and who have good English are now working in the Foreign Ministry or other agencies. Very few still serve as interpreters.

As a nation, we have been guilty of massive neglect of the study of foreign languages. Chinese in particular has suffered because of the hostile separation of the two nations for so many years. With opportunities for study and research now increasing in China and with contacts at all levels proliferating, we must develop a strong language program. It should begin at the high school level wherever possible and continue intensively through college and post-graduate studies with a view to training expert linguists as well as scholars in other China-related disciplines.

There is also a need for programs to train interpreters per se. Only a few institutions in the United States currently do so. The U.S. government does, but only for its own employees and even then interpreting is not seen as a career objective for its Foreign Service. Indeed, of the State Department's two Chinese interpreters, one is a Chinese-American who received her interpreter training in Europe after attending high school and college in the United States and the other is an American who went to high school in Taiwan. Neither is a foreign service officer. Georgetown University has a very good translating/interpreting program, but Chinese is not one of the languages offered. There are a few commercial courses, but one of my colleagues who enrolled in one wound up teaching most of the course!

The United States must do a better job of training and using Americans to translate and interpret Chinese. All too often over the past decade, Americans have relied on Chinese interpreters at meetings ranging from those between Mao Zedong and Richard Nixon down to visits of ordinary delegations. The National Committee believes that since Chinese hosts provide interpreters for American groups in China, it is incumbent upon the U.S. side to reciprocate by providing interpreters for its guests. This may also be a matter of pride; we should demonstrate that Americans can perform as competently as the excellent Chinese interpreters. In this regard, it is a step in the right direction that the State Department has finally hired two official American interpreters to sit at the negotiating table and take part in diplomatic functions.

But we need a new outlook which recognizes the vital importance of skilled interpreting not only in diplomacy, but also in many other areas, including commercial relations and cultural exchanges. This has been recognized for many years by those intimately concerned with the problem. What is lacking is the commitment to act on that recognition. The prospects for progress do not look good. If experience is an indicator of future trends, it may, unfortunately, be a long while before we begin systematically to produce the kind of interpreters we need.

Negotiations in China:
Observations of a Lawyer

STANLEY B. LUBMAN

Americans and other Westerners often say that commercial negotiations in China are difficult. Clearly, each side often has difficulty understanding the other. Clearly, negotiations in China seem to take longer than they might elsewhere. But why? It is easy to conclude that such difficulties are the natural result of the meeting of two disparate cultures. But the specific reasons for these problems, and the means of resolving them, take more effort to understand. Identifying some of the problems Westerners encounter in commercial negotiations in the People's Republic of China and isolating out certain unique characteristics of the Chinese-Western commercial negotiation may help us more fully comprehend some of the problems that tend to appear in the negotiating process.

The observations that follow are based on a decade of

participation, as a lawyer, in commercial negotiations with China. Since the negotiations were often intense, these observations out of necessity arose from fleeting perceptions and impressionistic reflections. They should, therefore, be critically examined. In addition, the negotiations in which my views were generated have usually involved large U.S. corporations, whose size and bureaucratic structure frequently made their representatives' style of doing business quite different from those of smaller, more nimble companies. Generalizations, then, should be considered critically in this light; obviously the nature and size of negotiating parties color the nature of the negotiations themselves.

The differences between Chinese and Westerners in commercial negotiations may exist at the most obvious levels—for example, the inability of each side to speak the other's language or grasp the subtleties of etiquette that each culture expects. The differences may also extend to less obvious but perhaps more significant disparities in the perception of the nature and implications of basic concepts, so that the two sides often appear to be talking *at,* rather than *with,* each other.

A specific illustration of such differences over fundamental legal concepts can be seen in negotiations over guarantees in licensing agreements. The language of guarantees to which the Chinese rigidly insist licensors agree is general and uncertain. Americans, on the other hand, demand specificity.

As one example, consider the standard clause used by the China National Technology Import Corporation, which states that products manufactured by the Chinese under a license from a foreign company shall meet a formal acceptance test. The essence of the guarantee clause is that if the results are unsatisfactory, the two sides should work at making it right; if ultimately they cannot do so they should jointly work out the consequences of that failure. These consequences may include payment of a penalty by the foreign side. The guarantee clause does not discuss the apportioning of specific rights and responsibilities, as an American guarantee clause would. Rather, it attempts to create a continuing obligation to repair a bad situation.

Although ultimately the clause could serve as the basis for an assertion by the Chinese of such rights as the right to a penalty or to a reduction in the contract price, the Chinese place stress on obtaining from the licensor the promised end-result rather than defining precisely the rights of parties involved. Hence rescission, the right to abrogate a contract, which is a standard remedy under Western contract law, is not contemplated by the Chinese clause. The result is an ambiguity which makes the Western negotiator uncomfortable.

The Chinese side, for instance, will ask for assurances that the licensor will do everything possible to insure that the product meets contract specifications, even if repeated and time-consuming tests involving the presence of the licensor's technicians in China are required. In response to this demand for a seemingly open-ended obligation, the American side will try to define an end to its obligations. After all, the unsatisfactory product may have resulted from the failure of the Chinese to follow technical instructions carefully, even though it may be difficult, if not impossible, to pinpoint their errors. The Chinese, on the other hand, may perceive the American position as an attempt to avoid responsibility for the Americans' own errors.

Part of the reason for the Chinese approach to contracts lies in their relatively limited experience with complicated commercial transactions. Until 1978, the China trade basically consisted of simple transactions: buying and selling goods that were packed and delivered in boxes, bales or containers. In recent years, however, China has become increasingly involved in more complex commercial activities. It is now interested, for example, in whole plant purchases, licenses of manufacturing technology, countertrade and joint ventures. These transactions are obviously larger and more complex than those of earlier times, and it stands to reason that the contracts involved should be more complicated. But the concepts associated with the simpler transactions have continued to pervade negotiations because the Chinese foreign trade corporations have persisted in using the old clauses and contracts with few or insufficient adaptations to the complexities of the newer commercial transactions. Likewise, some of the personnel who negotiate the current transactions have not yet been able to adjust to the new complexities.

Other disagreements in commercial negotiations stem from the absence of a common background or approach to solving problems. A striking contrast can be seen when the parties to the negotiation share a common vocabulary of concepts; when, for example, the discussions are between American and Chinese scientists and technicians who share a relatively high degree of common knowledge and experience.

In the dialogues of this sort that I have observed, both the Chinese and the Americans have been represented by scientists and engineers who understood well the technical problems they were to discuss, for example: the design and construction of an offshore oil drilling platform, the engineering of an iron mine, the manufacture of a scientific instrument, and so forth. Because of this body of common knowledge, relatively close rapport and mutual respect for technical competence developed quickly. Although the American and Chinese technicians were negotiating for advantageous commercial terms, their shared knowledge and professional vocabularies helped establish not only mutual respect and congeniality, but also a feeling (sometimes lacking in negotiations between trade officials and lawyers) of cooperating in a common enterprise. Thus both sides generally were able to rapidly establish the parameters of their discussion and plunge deeply into it. Past mistakes could be candidly admitted, discarded design alternatives reviewed, and specific applications of a product or service to the Chinese situation carefully examined.

In addition to the common knowledge and experience, other less obvious factors serve to ease tensions and facilitate discussion. Scientists and technicians hold high status in Chinese society. Lawyers and the law, by contrast, have been largely irrelevant until very recently in Chinese life. As a result, Chinese technicians and scientists are more apt to view their American counterparts as equals. This spirit of "egalitarianism" is also fostered by the fact that American and Chinese scientists and technicians have usually had similar educational backgrounds; in fact, some older Chinese were educated in the United States. Finally, U.S. and Chinese scientists and engineers are often less bound to the immediate commercial details of the negotiation at hand and are thus less prone to adopt an adversarial position than U.S. lawyers and Chinese trade officials.

Another contrast in the ability to establish rapport may be seen in negotiations in which PRC officials sit across the table from Overseas Chinese, who frequently display a different style of doing business from Westerners.

An obvious advantage that many Overseas Chinese enjoy is the ability to speak Chinese. The importance of a common language cannot be overemphasized. It is not merely a question of linguistic clarity. There are important cultural implications as well. Many Overseas Chinese, for instance, use forms of address and polite expressions which, though out of date in China today, continue to be respected as part of the Chinese cultural heritage. Not only can these forms of expression be used to soften the presentation of Western positions, but they also flatter the PRC representatives and help to create the feeling that all the ethnic Chinese in the room, regardless of their citizenship, are friends—if not relatives—who know how to go about creating a harmonious relationship.

Beyond this linguistic-cultural competence, many Overseas Chinese find it easier to establish rapport with PRC negotiators because their idea of doing business embraces a broader range of activities than that of Westerners. "Doing business" may extend to lavish entertaining and gift-giving—activities in which Americans, at least, tend to indulge less freely, especially since the adoption of the Foreign Corrupt Practices Act. This sort of entertaining and gift-giving has sometimes yielded undesirable results, and a number of well-publicized recent criminal prosecutions in China underscore the apprehensiveness of some authorities in the PRC about the potential for corruption involved. Nevertheless, some Western firms have been well served by persons of Chinese origin who socialize easily with their PRC counterparts and are successful in establishing personal relations and a sense of trust, but do not yield to some of the strong social pressures that can be exerted by the local Chinese on a company representative with whom they have much in common ethnically.

This kind of shared background and ability to establish rapport is often absent in negotiations between PRC officials, on the one hand, and American businessmen and lawyers, on the other. In particular, the American lawyer tends to be concerned about the issues and the contractual language related to defining the responsibilities and obligations of the two parties—with an eye toward the possibility of a breakdown in contractual relations. By contrast, Chinese negotiators are rarely lawyers, and they do not approach negotiations with the same kinds of questions and concerns. The Chinese view the contract as a *commercial* document which defines the desired outcome of the transaction; Westerners view the contract as a *legal* document which defines the responsibilities of parties to each other and to third persons and the consequent rights that each party enjoys.

Chinese negotiators are also often reluctant to consider the possibility of a breakdown in the relationship. The reasons for this lie in part in a cultural aversion to confronting openly the possibility of conflicts between parties. In addition, I am convinced that the Chinese side does not wish to engage in the time-consuming and no doubt impossible task of figuring out in advance the domestic Chinese bureaucratic consequences of a breakdown in contractual relations between the Chinese and foreign sides. At any rate, Chinese negotiators rarely welcome the foreign lawyer's concern over the possibility of conflict and the need to sort out the parties' rights, and are more often impatient when these concerns are aired.

This difference in basic concepts and attitudes has another consequence that tends to work against the establishment of rapport. Because they lack a common conceptual ground, each party tends to try to educate the other as to the proper way to proceed in a negotiation. Chinese negotiators, for example, often describe the process of approval of agreements within the Chinese bureaucracy and the requisite shape and form of such agreements as fixed and unalterable. Also, Chinese negotiators frequently assert that because they have already signed an agreement in one form with a foreign company, it should serve as a precedent for others. When the Western negotiators are skilled and experienced professionals, as is usually the case, this sort of on-the-job instruction can become quite irritating.

The didacticism of Chinese negotiators can be even more annoying to the foreign negotiator when he finds out that the Chinese are often unwilling to provide enlightenment on subjects that he considers important. For instance, if the foreign negotiator seeks to discuss reasons behind a Chinese position on pricing or other commercial terms, he may be informed that the position is dictated by internal and organizational considerations about which a foreigner should not be concerned. As a result, the foreign negotiator may feel that he is assumed to be ignorant, fated to remain so, and deserving of no special guidance on what are regarded as Chinese internal matters.

Some of these problems may be temporary in nature and should decrease as commercial contacts between China and the West grow. With the recent expansion of Chinese interest in importing technology, Chinese trade officials have acknowledged that their standard contract clauses will need modification. On the other hand, many of the problems noted above are traceable to cultural attitudes, which are hard indeed to change. As a result, much of the difficulty associated with commercial negotiations in China is likely to persist for some time.

Two other disparities in negotiation style are worth mentioning.

Chinese argumentation vs. U.S. argumentation. When Chinese negotiators state their position, explain and clarify it, and argue in its favor, their mode of exposition often seems to the American more repetitious, less complex and less well equipped with oratorical and argumentative flourishes than the argumentation employed by American negotiators. The Chinese side very often states its position, gives a few examples, offers a few justifications and rests its case. If they encounter opposition, Chinese negotiators tend to do no more than restate their original argument. It would be extraordinary for Chinese to change a major position without having discussed it among themselves first, which they will commonly do between negotiating sessions rather than by taking time out during a session.

American businessmen and lawyers, by contrast, if they encounter opposition to their point of view, will attempt by asking questions to elicit the reasoning behind the other side's position and will often engage in complex arguments intended to persuade the other side to change. An American negotiator may change his position in mid-argument or engage in variations on the original one, and may often be flexible enough to consult with his colleagues in mid-session and argue with them to change an original position.

These differences probably stem from the bureaucratic nature of the Chinese organizations involved. The Chinese negotiator's position has most likely been arrived at by a group, approved by his superiors within his own organization and perhaps also cleared with other organizations; as a result, his authority to vary from that position without prior consultation is extremely limited. Hence the repetition and the limited range of argumentation which seems characteristic of much Chinese negotiation, in contrast to the more independent style of American negotiators who usually possess more latitude.

"Overcomplex" foreign contracts vs. "oversimple" Chinese contracts. It is also common in Sino-American commercial negotiations for the Chinese side to arrive at the bargaining table either with no draft contract or with a simple, standard form contract that has been but little revised to fit the particular transaction involved. The U.S. side will usually be ready with a contract draft, but it will generally be based on standard contract forms of the U.S. company involved, forms heavily influenced by domestic situations and the complexity of the U.S. legal system and much too complicated for the Chinese. It happens that many U.S. contracts *are* prolix and very complicated, and therefore difficult for Chinese (they are not alone in this regard) to understand. The consequence is that often the Chinese insist, without having read the contract, that the U.S. side simplify it.

Even if the U.S. company has tried to pare down and simplify its contract, the Chinese side may continue to refuse to read it until it has again been shortened and even further simplified. Even with this additional simplification, the Chinese negotiators may still chide their U.S. counterparts for being wordy and legalistic. A Chinese trade negotiator with whom I have discussed these views has commented that another problem arises from the requirement on the Chinese side that the contract be approved by a higher-ranking official, who is likely to be less well-educated than the negotiators and therefore finds complicated contract clauses hard to understand.

As a result of these problems, contract negotiations often take the form of continuous Chinese assaults on a foreign draft that they allege to be unnecessarily complicated. If the foreign negotiators try to get the Chinese to propose a draft to serve as the basis for discussions, it will still seem incomplete compared with the American one. If the U.S. draft serves as the basis for discussion, by the end of negotiations it will be much skinnier and may have an extra arm or leg stuck on. If they start with the Chinese draft, it will be fatter than the original but no less ungainly.

Much more study is needed of the nature and causes of misunderstandings between Chinese and Americans in the context of commercial negotiations. Many other obvious influences on negotiations such as mistrust and ignorance have not been discussed here. In commercial negotiations, for instance, the failure of U.S. businessmen and lawyers to inform themselves about the Chinese economy and bureaucracy before they arrive in China often causes much wasted time and creates obstacles to understanding.

Moreover, the need for study of problems in Sino-American negotiations extends beyond commerce. There is room for fruitful analysis of diplomatic negotiations and of negotiations on scientific and cultural exchanges. Social scientists and lawyers have in recent years devoted considerable attention to the negotiating process, and insights drawn from their research could probably be usefully applied to Sino-Western negotiations. In the meantime, negotiators on both sides of the Pacific will continue to labor in their present unscientific manner, often bemused by the complex differences in culture, language and national character that produce difficulties in Sino-American negotiations.

A final note: many times the common effort to solve these problems creates bonds between the two sides. Consider a banquet lunch to which an American group representing a U.S. corporation had invited their Chinese opposite numbers. The leader of the American delegation welcomed the Chinese to the lunch, which he announced as a celebration of "Groundhog Day." The Chinese interpreter didn't know how to translate "groundhog," and neither did I. After we all figured out that a groundhog was small, brown, furry, lived in a hole and could be eaten, a very good time was had by all.

The Importance of Being KEQI:
A Note on Communication Difficulties

YAO WEI

We all know that words in one language can be very difficult to translate into another. Is there something beyond language that at times makes communicating so difficult? English and Chinese are a case in point. The exact meaning of words like "kicks," "ambition," "privacy" and so on are not that easily translated into Chinese. On the other hand, Chinese words are tremendously difficult to translate into English.

I think one has to bear in mind that a given language is always a part, sometimes a very important part, of a given civilization. Like civilization, it has its roots in the past and will continue to grow in the future. The Chinese word (or "term" rather) *keqi* (客氣) is a good example. There is no single word in English that can adequately define it. Yet, without understanding what *keqi* really means, one is certain to miss the *Chinese-ness* in and perhaps even totally misunderstand many

71

transactions taking place every day.

Ke in Chinese means "guest," and *qi* means "air" or "behavior." Put together, it means "behavior of a guest." *Keqi* can, therefore, mean polite, courteous, modest, humble, understanding, considerate, well-mannered, etc. It cannot be enveloped by any single English word; it is the synthesis of many. Yet, one hears the term more often used in the grammatically negative form, *bukeqi* (不客氣) or *buyao keqi* (不要客氣), which is "Don't be *keqi*." But any of the above English versions if used in the negative would create misunderstanding, unless a "too" or "over" is added after "Don't be . . . ." For instance, "Don't be too polite" or "Don't be overmodest." Actually, "Don't stand on ceremony" would be a better translation of *buyao keqi*. However "too" or "over" would create problems if used when translating the affirmative form. *Ta duiwo hen keqi* (他對我很客氣) means "He is very kind to me" and certainly not "He is standing on too much ceremony with me."

In the Chinese dictionary, *keqi* is further defined as "having *limao*" (禮貌), which means "politeness." But again, the Chinese *limao* is not entirely "politeness" in the English sense. From childhood, the Chinese are taught *lijiao* (禮教), usually translated "ethical education." In the past this was often done by reciting from the classics under the harsh tutelage of a master; nowadays children learn by word of mouth from parents and grandparents. One can trace the roots of *li* or "rites" to the Zhou period, which is roughly 1066-221 B.C. In reality, much present-day behavior can easily be linked to that distant past.

To be humble is an important facet of *keqi*. But, once again, this humbleness extends far beyond the "humbleness" of what is meant by that word in this country. As a part of *keqi,* to be humble means that you not only have to be humble yourself but also make anybody or anything related to you a part of your humbleness. That is why one often hears from a Chinese disapproving remarks of his children and of the people working under him. He fears that anything positive he says may be construed as arrogance or haughtiness or just being without *li*.

Americans tend to be much more assertive than the ordinary Chinese. To assert oneself is certainly no breach of propriety in the United States. As a matter of fact, assertiveness is an important feature of the society here. Just look at the advertisements! But assertiveness of an individual is still often viewed as lacking *li* or at least not very *keqi* by most Chinese. This is reflected in the language. If a Chinese comes here to live and work, probably the very first thing he has to learn in order to survive is to assert himself. Otherwise he will not even be able to exist. If a first-rate Chinese carpenter went to a furniture company to find work, the interview dialogue would probably be something like this:

Employer: Have you done carpentry work before?

Carpenter: I don't dare to say I have. I have just been in a very modest way involved in the carpenter trade.

Employer: What are you skilled in then?

Carpenter: I won't say "skilled." I have only a little experience in making tables [although he may have been making all kinds of tables for the past twenty-five years].

Employer: Can you make something now and show us how good you are?

Carpenter: How dare I be so indiscreet as to demonstrate my crude skills in front of a master of the trade like you?

By this time the employer might just be fed up and say "I'm sorry but we don't take novices" and show him the door. But, if the employer is more subtle and persistent, the carpenter would probably respond: "If you really insist, I'll try to make a table.

Please don't laugh at my crude work.'' With that he commences to work on a table, saying a few more times "Please don't laugh at my crude work . . .'' and gives the final touches to a perhaps beautiful piece of art in the shape of a table.

Of course, things are beginning to change, and with them the meaning of *keqi*. But, whatever the changes, continuities can still be found in the conduct of everyday life in China as well as among many Chinese living abroad. When an American happens to arrive at a Chinese family's home at dinnertime, nine times out of ten he will be asked (sometimes even in a rather compelling way) to eat with the family. At the table, he will be served by the host (or hostess), usually giving the appearance of being force-fed. The same with liquor: a host with *li* will pay a great deal of attention to filling your glass and will keep on toasting you. While this kind of hospitality might make an American uncomfortable, a Chinese would feel ill at ease or hesitant to eat to the full when invited to a dinner where the host is less insistent. Of course, "Dutch treat" would be unthinkable to most Chinese even to this day. To the Chinese, greeting and seeing people off must certainly be at the door. Anything less would be lacking, if not devoid of *li*. Our late Premier Zhou Enlai always made it a point to do just that, whether his guest was a head of state or an ordinary newspaper reporter.

Of course not all problems are at this level; simple linguistic misunderstandings often occur as well. One problem is that too many ordinary, everyday English words now have a sexual connotation not found even in the most comprehensive dictionary. A friend once came to the United States with a delegation and, in the course of the visit which lasted for about a month, learned some simple English words and expressions, like "How are you?" "My best wishes to your wife and family," "Bottoms up!" and so forth. At the last dinner party given by

74

some bankers at a coastal city, to the amazement of the Americans at the table, he stood up, glass in hand, and toasted the host: "I wish your wife bottoms up!" It took some time to explain to him the "bottom" and "top" usage other than their more innocent forms. People here tend to prefer to use the word "rooster" rather than "cock," "merry" rather than "gay" and "transaction" rather than "intercourse," but how is the English language student in China to know? To communicate better, I think we all should be more accommodating and understanding or perhaps be a little *keqi*?

Suggestions for Further Reading

A wealth of material awaits anyone wishing to do further reading on China. Suggested here is a small sample of the items available, and each has its own bibliography offering new leads.

General Background

For a general account of recent Chinese history, the fourth edition of John King Fairbank's *The United States and China* (Cambridge, MA: Harvard University Press, 1979) is a good place to start. *The People's Republic of China: A Basic Handbook,* compiled by Richard Bush and James Townsend (New York: Learning Resources in International Studies, 1982) provides a wealth of facts and figures in a compact form. *The Cambridge Encyclopedia of China* (New York: Cambridge University Press, 1982), under the general editorship of Brian Hook, and

Encyclopedia of China Today (Third Edition; New York: Harper & Row and Eurasia Press, 1981), edited by Frederic M. Kaplan and Julian M. Sobin, are useful reference volumes. The latter emphasizes the contemporary period while the former takes in all of Chinese civilization. *China Under the Four Modernizations,* a collection of papers sponsored by the Joint Economic Committee of the U.S. Congress (Washington, DC: Government Printing Office, 1982), is the best single work on the Chinese economy. Victor Li's *Law Without Lawyers* (Boulder, CO: Westview Press, 1980) describes the system of criminal justice and social control.

Recently, there have appeared a number of books that open windows on the complexities of Chinese social and political life. Among the better ones are David Bonavia, *The Chinese* (New York: Lippincott & Crowell, 1980), B. Michael Frolic, *Mao's People: Sixteen Portraits of Life in Revolutionary China* (Cambridge, MA: Harvard University Press, 1980), Roger Garside, *Coming Alive!: China After Mao* (New York: McGraw Hill, 1981), and Fox Butterfield, *China: Alive in the Bitter Sea* (New York: Times Books, 1982). The short stories in *Chinese Literature,* published in the PRC, often explore the subtleties of social relations in China.

Background on Sino-American and Sino-Western Relations

Jerome Chen explores a century of Sino-Western social and cultural contacts in his *China and the West* (Bloomington, IN: Indiana University, 1979), and Michael Schaller's *The United States and China in the Twentieth Century* (New York: Oxford University, 1979) is a good one-volume introduction. Harold Isaacs explores the evolution of shifting American attitudes toward China and the Chinese in *Scratches on Our Minds* (White Plains, NY: M. E. Sharpe, 1980). For the continuing Chinese ambivalence about the outside world, see Orville Schell's *Watch*

Out for the Foreign Guests (New York: Pantheon, 1980). The historical context of contemporary U.S.-China relations is presented in John Fairbank's *China: The People's Middle Kingdom and the United States* (Cambridge, MA: Harvard University Press, 1967) and *Dragon and Eagle, United States-China Relations: Past and Future* (New York: Basic Books, Inc, 1978) edited by Michel Oksenberg and Robert B. Oxnam. Harry Harding presents an agenda of policy issues in current U.S.-China relations in his *China and the U.S.: Normalization and Beyond* (New York: Foreign Policy Association, 1979). The bimonthly *China Business Review,* published by the National Council for U.S.-China Trade, provides sound, up-to-date information on developments in the Chinese economy and U.S.-China trade. *China Exchange News,* published quarterly by the Washington-based Committee on Scholarly Communication with the PRC, does the same for science and education.

Communicating with China

On the Chinese language itself, *The Chinese Language Today* by Paul Kratochvil (London: Hutchinson & Co., 1968) is a comprehensive and readable introduction. *Language and Linguistics in the PRC* (Austin, TX: University of Texas Press, 1975), edited by Winfred P. Lehmann, is the report of post-1949 developments by a delegation of linguistic specialists, while *Language Reform in China: Documents and Commentary* (White Plains, NY: M. E. Sharpe, 1979) offers a collection of Chinese opinions on those changes. Chiang Yee's *Chinese Calligraphy,* third edition (Cambridge, MA: Harvard University Press, 1973) is a Chinese intellectual's analysis and admiration of the traditional script.

The experiences of Westerners who spent extended periods of time in China can often shed light on the problems of intercultural communication. Jonathan Spence's *To Change China: Western Advisers in China, 1620-1900* (Boston: Little, Brown, 1969) offers capsule accounts of some. Examples of individual memoirs are George N. Kates, *The Years That Were Fat: The Last of Old China (Cambridge, MA: MIT Press, 1967)*, Graham Peck, *Two Kinds of Time* (Boston: Houghton Mifflin, 1968), and Austin Coates, *Myself a Mandarin* (Hong Kong: Heinemann Educational Books, n.d.)

Of a more practical nature, *China Guidebook: 1982-83 Edition* by Arne J. deKeijzer and Frederic M. Kaplan is much more than the usual tourist aid. And the U.S.-China Education Clearinghouse has prepared a set of useful materials. Among them are *An Introduction to Education in the People's Republic of China and U.S.-China Educational Exchanges* by Thomas Fingar and Linda A. Reed, *China Bound: A Handbook for American Students, Researchers and Teachers* by Karen Turner Gottschang, and *Assisting Students and Scholars from the People's Republic of China: A Handbook for Community Groups* by Katherine C. Donovan. All are available from the National Association for Foreign Student Affairs in Washington, DC.